.oh
joy!

JOY CHO

.oh
joy!

60 WAYS TO CREATE & GIVE JOY

WILLIAM MORROW
An Imprint of HarperCollinsPublishers

Also by Joy Cho
Blog, Inc.
Creative, Inc.

HarperCollins books may be purchased for educational, business, or
sales promotional use. For information please e-mail the Special Markets
Department at SPsales@harpercollins.com.

FIRST EDITION

Creative Direction by Joy Cho
Photographs by Casey Brodley
Design by Angie Stalker
Styling and Crafts by Julia Wester

Library of Congress Cataloging-in-Publication Data has been applied for.

ISBN 978-0-06-234448-9

15 16 17 18 19 IDCC/QG 10 9 8 7 6 5 4 3 2 1

Thank you to everyone who has read my blog for however long you've been reading— whether years, months, or days. Your support and enthusiasm makes me even more excited to do what I do and to be inspired to share my vision of the world with all of you.

CONTENTS

When I started my blog in 2005, I had no idea that I'd be connecting with actual, live people around the world who would since become loyal readers who have helped shape Oh Joy! into what it is today. Through my website, I've been able to share my view of the world and the types of things I love most—food, fashion, home decor—as well as various parts of my life. As I celebrate a decade of blogging, I'm excited to share these brand-new, original projects that I hope will add a little Oh Joy! to your daily life as well.

This book gives insight into my creative process and tips for bringing more color and whimsy into your day. With the DIY projects, I encourage you to create them for entertaining, as gifts, and simply to make every day a little happier. Enjoy!

COLOR

It's hard to imagine that there was a time when I dressed in only black and gray. I moved from the East Coast to Southern California in 2009, and it was like I was always meant to be here. The sunshine, the flowers, the buildings, and the vibrancy that surrounds me inspired my taste and style from the moment I began calling Los Angeles my home. These days, I barely wear any black or gray and when I do, my friends ask me if something is wrong!

When it comes to color, I am all about embracing it, whether it's wearing it or decorating with it. But you need to feel comfortable—not everyone is ready to throw a whole bunch of colors together and call it a day—so here are a few tips on how I like to mix colors together.

There's a palette I love using that I tend to call Fruit Salad on Acid. It's a mix of soft and fruity colors kicked up a notch.

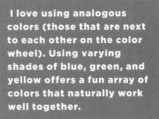
I love using analogous colors (those that are next to each other on the color wheel). Using varying shades of blue, green, and yellow offers a fun array of colors that naturally work well together.

J B

PATTERN

I really came to love pattern while working for fashion designer Cynthia Rowley in one of my first jobs out of school. I was surrounded by confident women dressed in head-to-toe pattern and loved how they embraced mix-and-match in a new way. I was in my early twenties and trying to figure out not only my style but my whole direction in life, in general—and the experience really inspired me in how to dress and bring pattern into my everyday life.

Although patterns by definition include a recurring image on repeat, play with icons, too (like the camel on this pillow), that add even more whimsy to the mix.

When you mix two patterns, one should be a little more simple, so that you're not creating an optical illusion: for example, the simplicity of the dress pattern over the more fanciful hand pattern. Using two patterns with an overlapping color helps tie them together while giving the eyes room to breathe.

Using two patterns with an overlapping color helps tie them together while giving the eyes room with breathe with the simplicity of the dress pattern over the more fanciful hand pattern.

When mixing two patterns, one should be a little more simple, so that you're not creating an optical illusion.

WHIMSY

To be whimsical is to be playful or fanciful. There's almost always an opportunity to add whimsy to your life, from the gifts you make for others, to the way you dress, to the things you do to make your home feel special. Making something whimsical is simply a matter of adding an element or two that makes someone smile. Is it a patterned lining underneath a neutral coat, a surprise message inside a cookie, or a fruit salad made with letter-shaped fruit?

Art prints and interesting vessels can give that extra wink to any room. If it makes you smile, it will make others smile, too.

Add flowers in unexpected places for an organic and blooming surprise for any celebration.

Both sparkling and unexpected, a few vintage brooches pinned to a sweatshirt adds instant wearable whimsy.

CREATING A COLOR PALETTE

Earlier in the book, I shared a few of my favorite color palettes. But how do you create a color palette for a project that feels perfect for you? The easiest way is to pull out photos, illustrations, or artwork you love from your favorite magazines and books, and websites like Pinterest. Take a look at the images that draw you in, then use the main colors as inspiration to pick out fabrics to make a pillow, wall paint for a room in your house, or flowers for a surprise bouquet.

DOTTY WALL ART

FOR A TEMPORARY AND TEXTURAL WAY TO DECORATE A ROOM, TRY FILLING UP A CORNER OR A WHOLE WALL WITH THESE PLAYFUL YARN DOTS!

1. Pin the cardstock circles where you'd like them to go on the wall.

2. Place pushpins evenly around the outside of each circle. Remove the paper circle.

3. Decide what color yarn you'll use and start stringing! If you imagine the circle like a clock, begin by securing a knot on the top pushpin at 12 o'clock, then loop the string around a pin at 5 o'clock, then diagonally back to 11 o'clock, then to 4 o'clock, to 10 o'clock, and so on.

4. Keep going counterclockwise until you've gone around twice to create a nice dense area of color.

5. Repeat to make the remaining string circles.

THREAD OR YARN IN YOUR CHOICE OF COLORS

GOLD TACKS

CARDSTOCK CUT INTO CIRCLES IN YOUR PREFERRED SIZE (WE USED THREE DIAMETERS 4-, 6- AND 8-INCH)

TWISTS ON THE EVERYDAY

I'm a big fan of trying new things, even if they're just variations on what we already know. We have amazing produce in California, and I always find myself so inspired after coming across the bounty of fruit available at my local farmers' market in L.A. Gems like these golden raspberries, green figs, and cherriums (a mix of a cherry and a plum!) take me outside my comfort zone of what's expected and make even the simplest snack more special.

EDIBLE CONFETTI

1. Using a standard hole punch, pop out mini circles of various leafy vegetables, herb leaves, and fruit skins.

2. Add fruit and mint to ice cubes for a summery drink or give cream cheese and dips an extra kick with citrus and veggies!

WE USED CARROTS, BASIL, MINT, RED CABBAGE, AND BUTTERNUT SQUASH

HOLE PUNCH

STRIPED OMBRÉ CAKE

PRETTY UP A SIMPLE CAKE WITH A TECHNIQUE THAT'S
BOTH BEAUTIFUL AND EDIBLE.

FINE SIEVE

STRIPED OMBRÉ CAKE (RECIPE PAGE 178)

SCISSORS OR X-ACTO KNIFE

CARDSTOCK

1. Make the base cake, using our recipe.

2. In a spice or coffee grinder, blend the fruit to a fine powder.

3. Pour the fruit powder into a bowl and whisk with some powdered sugar to loosen up any clumps. Sift the mixture through a mesh sieve to remove any large pieces.

4. Divide into 5 small dishes and gradually add more powdered sugar to create a gradient of shades, from the most red to less red to white.

5. Cut cardstock into even strips (½-inch strips are shown on an 8-inch round cake)

6. Lay the first strip of paper and a larger sheet parallel to it. The space between will equal the width of your stripe.

7. Sift the first color in the open area, then move the large cardstock and strip over to create the next stripe, making sure to change the color after 1 or 2 stripes.

8. Repeat across the whole cake.

TO STORE THE FRUIT AND SUGAR MIXTURE, KEEP IT DRY IN AN AIRTIGHT CONTAINER OR SMALL PLASTIC BAG.

FREEZE-DRIED CRANBERRIES (YOU CAN USE OTHER FRUIT TO CREATE DIFFERENT COLORS)

PUFFY PATTERN WRAP

1. Choose your wrapping paper; solid colors work best. You can even use simple white or kraft paper or the inside of a flattened paper grocery bag.

2. Wrap the gift with the paper as you usually would, but be sure to use double-sided tape to secure the ends so there's no tape on the exterior of the package.

3. Use the puffy paints to make the pattern or drawing of your choice on the top of the package. Let dry, and then move on to decorate the sides. Keep going until you've covered at least the sides that show.

4. Let dry completely (at least a few hours to overnight), then add a simple ribbon or button to the top if you'd like!

SOLID WRAPPING PAPER

DOUBLE-SIDED GIFT-WRAPPING TAPE

PUFFY PAINT IN THE COLORS OF YOUR CHOICE

28

FLORAL FRIENDS

One of my favorite things to collect is quirky vessels—shaped like animals or people—that on their own are pretty cute, but with flowers added become even more lively.

BAUBLE KEY CHAIN

WE CARRY AROUND A KEY CHAIN EVERY DAY, SO MAKE A CUTE AND CUSTOMIZABLE ONE FOR YOURSELF OR AS A GIFT.

GALVANIZED CABLE WIRE

NEON CORD (PARACHUTE CORD 325)

DUCT TAPE

GOLD EMBROIDERY ROPE

SNAP HOOK KEY RING IN GOLD

HOT GLUE

SPRAY PAINT IN COLOR OF YOUR CHOICE

DRILL AND 1/16-INCH DRILL BIT

TO MAKE THE BASE RING

1. Cut the cable wire to 1½ feet.

2. Hook the snap hook key ring onto the wire, as well as the split ring that will eventually hold the keys.

3. Wrap the wire into a circle so that it doubles up and secure by wrapping duct tape around the entire circled wire.

4. Cut about 4 feet of neon cord and gold embroidery rope and wrap them around the main wire ring.

5. Use a hot glue gun to secure the end of the rope to the wire ring and continue to glue as you wrap the rope. Keep wrapping until you reach the end, then secure with hot glue.

TO ATTACH LETTERS OR BEADS

1. To attach a letter, use the ½-inch gold split ring to hook through the decorative plastic letter and attach onto the base ring. If you have a letter without an existing hole (say, a J or a T), you can glue the letter onto another base, such as a flat bead with an existing hole.

2. To attach a bead, loop the orange elastic cord through the decorative base ring you just made and tie a knot at the end of the cord close to the base ring. Thread both ends of the cord into the bead and tie another knot at the end of the bead.

TO MAKE THE ANIMAL KEY CHAIN

1. Spray paint the plastic animal in the color of your choice.

2. Drill a hole using 1/16-inch drill bit. It should be just deep enough so you can screw in the eye hook by hand—the hole should not go all the way through.

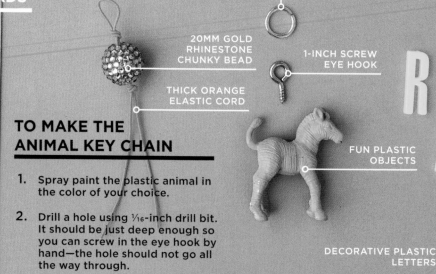

½-INCH GOLD SPLIT RING

20MM GOLD RHINESTONE CHUNKY BEAD

1-INCH SCREW EYE HOOK

THICK ORANGE ELASTIC CORD

FUN PLASTIC OBJECTS

DECORATIVE PLASTIC LETTERS

FRUITY STICKY NOTES

SURPRISE SOMEONE WITH AN UNEXPECTED MESSAGE ON
THEIR DAILY DOSE OF FRUIT AND VEGGIES.

1. Print the templates onto the label paper of your choice (I used gold paper).

2. Cut out the stickers and place them onto fruit or veggies for a sweet message.

FRUIT AND VEGGIES

YOU'RE FRESH

LABEL PAPER

SO GOOD

PICK ME!

I CHEWS YOU!

TEMPLATES (PAGE 189)

A SWEET TREAT!

SO GOOD

YOU'RE FRESH

CHEW ON THIS

A SWEET TREAT!

I CHEWS YOU!

PICK ME!

SO GOOD

YOU'RE FRESH

CHEW ON THIS

A SWEET TREAT!

I CHEWS YOU!

PICK ME!

SO GOOD

YOU'RE FRESH

CHEW ON THIS

A SWEET TREAT!

I CHEWS YOU!

PICK ME!

SO GOOD

YOU'RE FRESH

CHEW ON THIS

A SWEET TREAT!

I CHEWS YOU!

PICK ME!

PICK ME!

SO GOOD

YOU'RE FRESH

CHEW ON THIS

A SWEET TREAT!

I CHEWS YOU!

PICK ME!

PIC M

PI M

PIC

SCISSORS OR X-ACTO KNIFE

VINTAGE ITEMS FOR YOUR HOME

I love collecting vintage things—from quirky decorative objects and bowls to pretty brooches and hairpins. They're items I continue to add to incorporate regularly into my wardrobe and home. When buying vintage, here are a few things to keep in mind:

1. Make sure the pieces are in good shape. You might find a piece you love, but if it's rusted or damaged beyond the point of no return, you won't get much use out of it.

2. Get pieces you can actually use. If they're in good quality, you should still be able to wear them, serve out of them, or decorate with them. No one wants to buy something only to have it sit in a box, unappreciated.

3. The piece should make you smile. It should feel like something you can't buy online or on the shelf of an ordinary store. Make sure it feels fun and special.

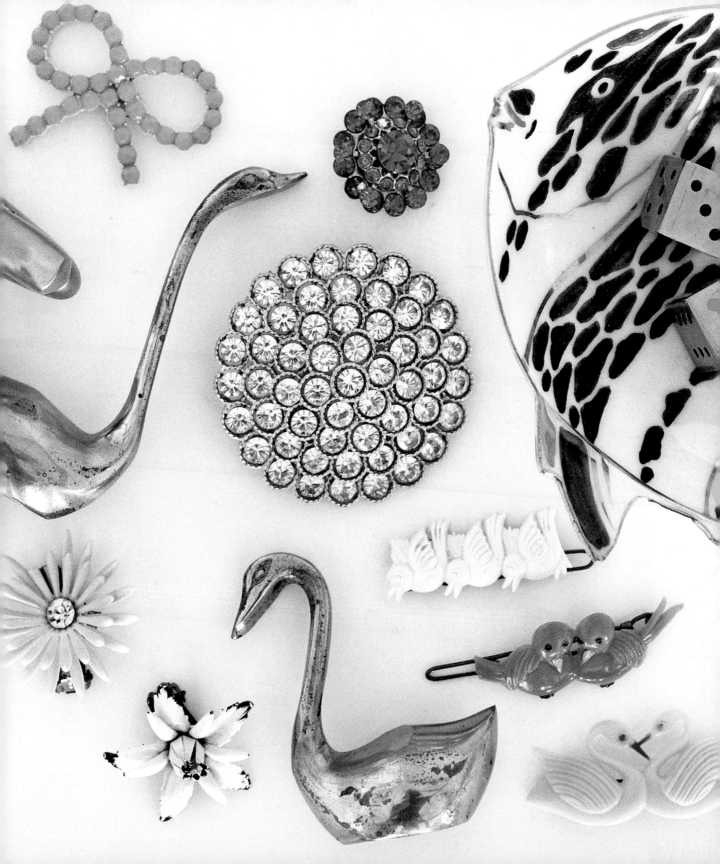

BABY SHOE-RARIUM

TURN THAT PRECIOUS FIRST PAIR OF BABY SHOES INTO A WHIMSICAL PIECE THAT YOU'LL LOVE TO DISPLAY FOR YEARS TO COME.

BABY SHOES

SUPERGLUE

PLEXIGLAS BOX WITH LID

MINI DECORATIONS OF
YOUR CHOICE, SUCH
AS VINTAGE CUPCAKE
TOPPERS, SMALL TOYS,
TINY PLANTS OR TREES

MINI WORDS OR
LETTERS

FAUX GRASS

1. Find a box that will fit your baby shoes with
   enough space around them for some tiny
   decorations.

2. Cut faux grass to fit the bottom of the box.

3. Set the grass on a work surface and set the
   shoes where you'd like them to be placed.

4. Place the mini decorations around the shoes
   to suit your fancy. Secure the shoes and other
   items with super glue when you've decided on
   the final placement.

5. Add letters or a name if you choose!

THROW A PILLOW PARTY!

Remember why slumber parties were so great when you were a kid? It's because you got to hang out on the floor, eat lots of fun food, stay up late, and treat your living room like a giant bed! Re-create that kind of fun with a pillow party in your living room by tossing every pillow you own on the ground. Have each guest bring a couple of pillows to add to the mix. Now your living room is like an indoor picnic that's super fun and casual. Finally, add food (or treats!) of your choice!

MAGIC FORTUNE JAR

MAKE AND GIVE YOUR VERY OWN FORTUNE-TELLER FOR A WITTY GIFT AND INSTANT CONVERSATION PIECE.

ADHESIVE FOAM SHEET

STYROFOAM BALL

GLASS JAR WITH LID

heck yeah!

WASHI TAPE

PERMANENT MARKER

CONTACT PAPER

1. Use the box template (page 190) to cut out a foam cube.

2. Press down on the Styrofoam ball to create the top, bottom, and sides of a cube. Use a butter knife to cut down the rounded sides into a cube.

3. Write 6 words or phrases of your choice, one on each side of the box, with a permanent marker.

4. Remove the adhesive back from the foam sheet and press the sheet around the Styrofoam cube to create the fortune cube. Press to adhere well.

5. Decorate the jar with washi tape.

6. Add the cube to the jar. Fill the jar with water until the cube floats to the top, leaving enough air at the top so the cube floats to the bottom of the jar when it's turned upside down. Seal the jar and test the water level; adjust as necessary.

CHOOSING ART FOR YOUR HOME

Since I love so many kinds of art (from photos to paintings to prints), I have a hard time sticking to just one style. And the best thing is, you don't have to choose just one type of artwork to hang on the wall. When collecting or gathering art for your home—whether spread out into various areas of one room or all together on a single gallery wall—there are a few things to keep in mind to help the pieces work together without being too matchy-matchy.

Choose a general color palette in the art. While you don't need to stick to very specific colors, all the pieces in one room (or on one wall) should generally contain some of the same colors. Even if an item is very colorful, make sure there are some colors that cross into other pieces.

Mix and match frames. Sometimes people think they need to have the same color frames throughout their whole home. I say stick to a few different frame colors and let those be the ones you generally turn to. Similar to the color palette mentioned above, a few black frames in a sea of gold and white frames works as long as there are enough to balance out the weight of color.

Find a general tone or feeling that unites your art. If you like to cross mediums as I do, the feeling of the art helps to make it all work together, whether photo, print, or painting. I tend to like art that is whimsical and colorful, and makes you smile in some way. These qualities attract me to certain pieces, which then inherently go together.

GLOW ON

ILLUMINATE ANY AREA WITH THIS CUSTOMIZABLE NEON SIGN.

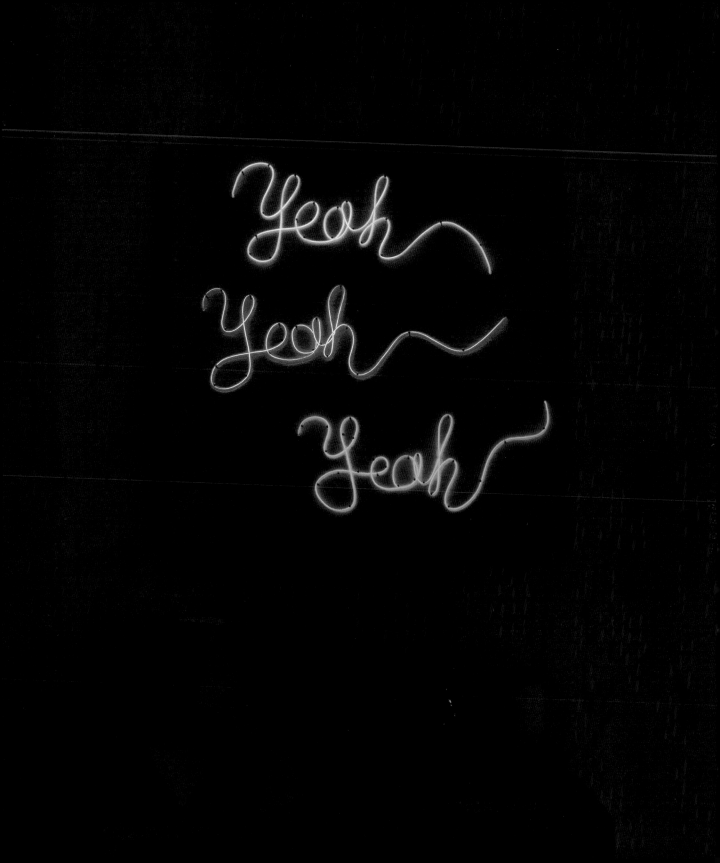

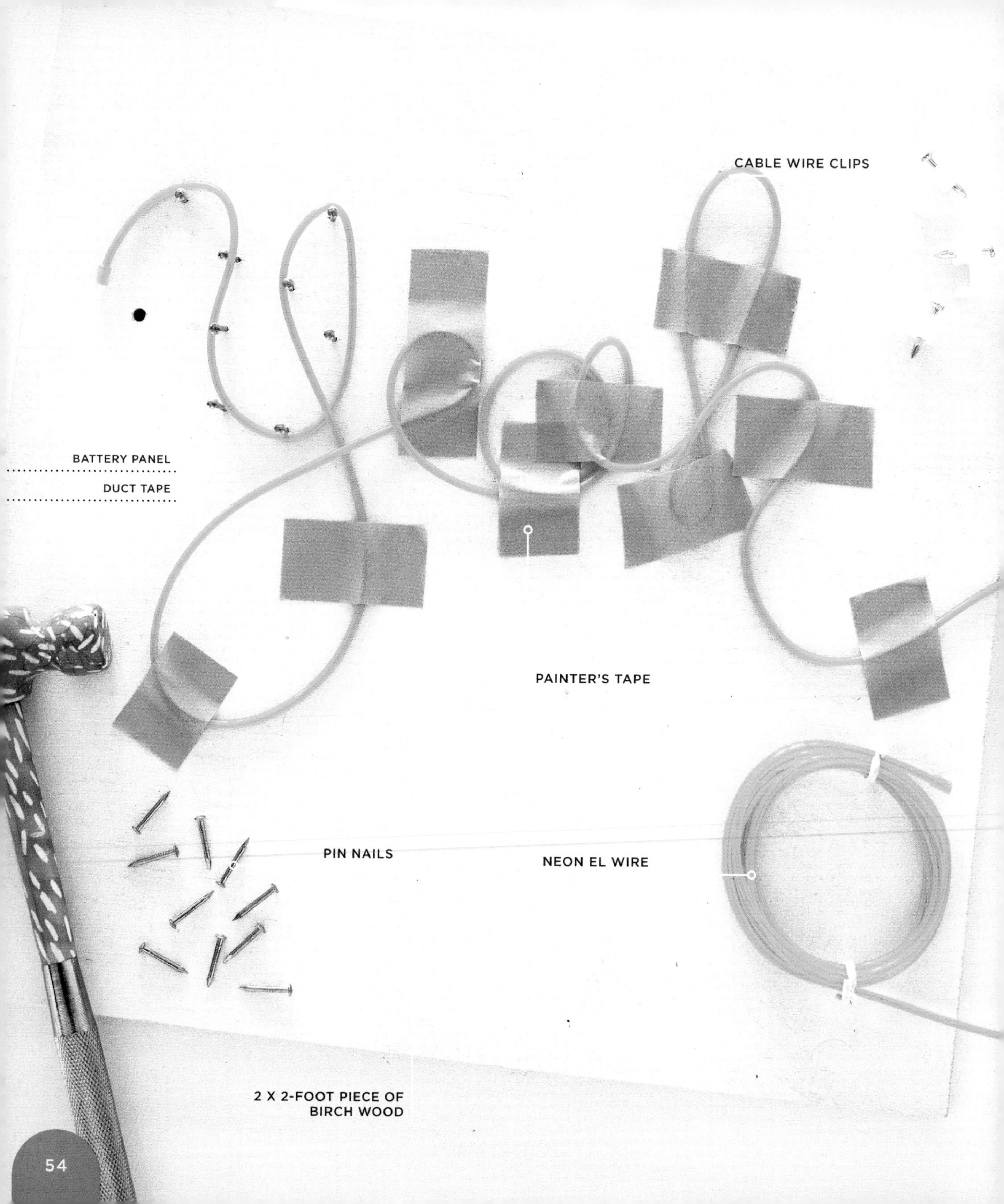

CABLE WIRE CLIPS

BATTERY PANEL

DUCT TAPE

PAINTER'S TAPE

PIN NAILS

NEON EL WIRE

2 X 2-FOOT PIECE OF
BIRCH WOOD

1. Decide what word or phrase you'll write.

2. String the neon wire onto the wood board to spell out the text.

3. Use painter's tape to secure the word to the wood board, then nail pin nails along alternating sides of the letter to secure the wire onto the board. Remove the tape as you go.

4. Drill a hole at the beginning of the word, where the wire starts, and another hole at the opposite end of the word, where it ends.

5. Remove the wire and string the wire through the hole from right to left, starting from the back of the board, and thread to re-create the word back through the nails.

6. Secure the beginning of the wire in the hole at the beginning of the word. Be sure to drill each hole at the end of each word, giving enough room for all the wires to connect in the back and into the battery panel.

7. Use duct tape to tape the battery panel to the lower-middle portion of the board so you can reach it easily to turn it on and off.

8. Secure the wires to the back with cable wire clips to keep them neat and in place.

FLORAL POP PRINT

CUSTOMIZE A FAVORITE PHOTO BY ADDING A 3-D FLORAL TWIST!

1. Print out a photo in your desired size onto photo paper.

2. Use a Styrofoam glue or strong paper glue to secure the photo onto the Styrofoam.

3. Remove the glass and backing from the frame. Place the photo with the Styrofoam into the frame. It should fit pretty snugly.

4. Use a small scissors to poke holes where you'd like to place the flowers on the photo.

5. Trim small flowers to desired length and insert into areas of the photo to accent the image.

6. When you've decided on final placement of the flowers, dab superglue on the backs of the flowers and secure them in the little holes.

A ½-INCH-THICK
SHEET OF STYROFOAM
THE SAME SIZE AS
YOUR PHOTO

A PHOTO OF
YOUR CHOICE

FRAME TO FIT
THE PHOTO

SMALL SCISSORS

STYROFOAM GLUE OR
STRONG PAPER GLUE

SUPERGLUE

SILK OR PAPER FLOWERS

SURPRISE SOMEONE

Everyone likes a good surprise, but the best ones happen when you least expect it—not on a birthday or otherwise special occasion. I love the idea of inserting a surprise into an everyday moment (like the fruity sticky notes on page 34 or the hanger notes on page 62). Why not create something even bigger from time to time by adding flowers to an otherwise gritty corner or balloons at someone's doorstep?

MINI PHOTO BLOCK PUZZLE

TURN A PRIZED PHOTO INTO A GIFT BY MAKING AN INTERACTIVE BLOCK SET THAT CAN ALSO MAKE A FUN SURPRISE TO SEND IN THE MAIL.

A PHOTO THAT WILL LOOK GOOD IN A SQUARE FORMAT

MAILING TUBE

NINE 1-INCH WOODEN BLOCKS

CLEAR GESSO

1. Print the photo so that you have a 3 x 3-inch image area. Cut the photo into nine 1-inch square pieces.

2. Brush gesso on one side of a block, then brush gesso on the back of one photo section and set it in place on the block. Repeat with the other 8 blocks.

3. Let set for 24 hours.

4. Place the blocks in a cardboard mailer and send them to someone who will be delighted!

HANGER NOTES

BE BRIGHT

HIGH FIVE!

RISE AND SHINE!

HEY GOOD LOOKIN'

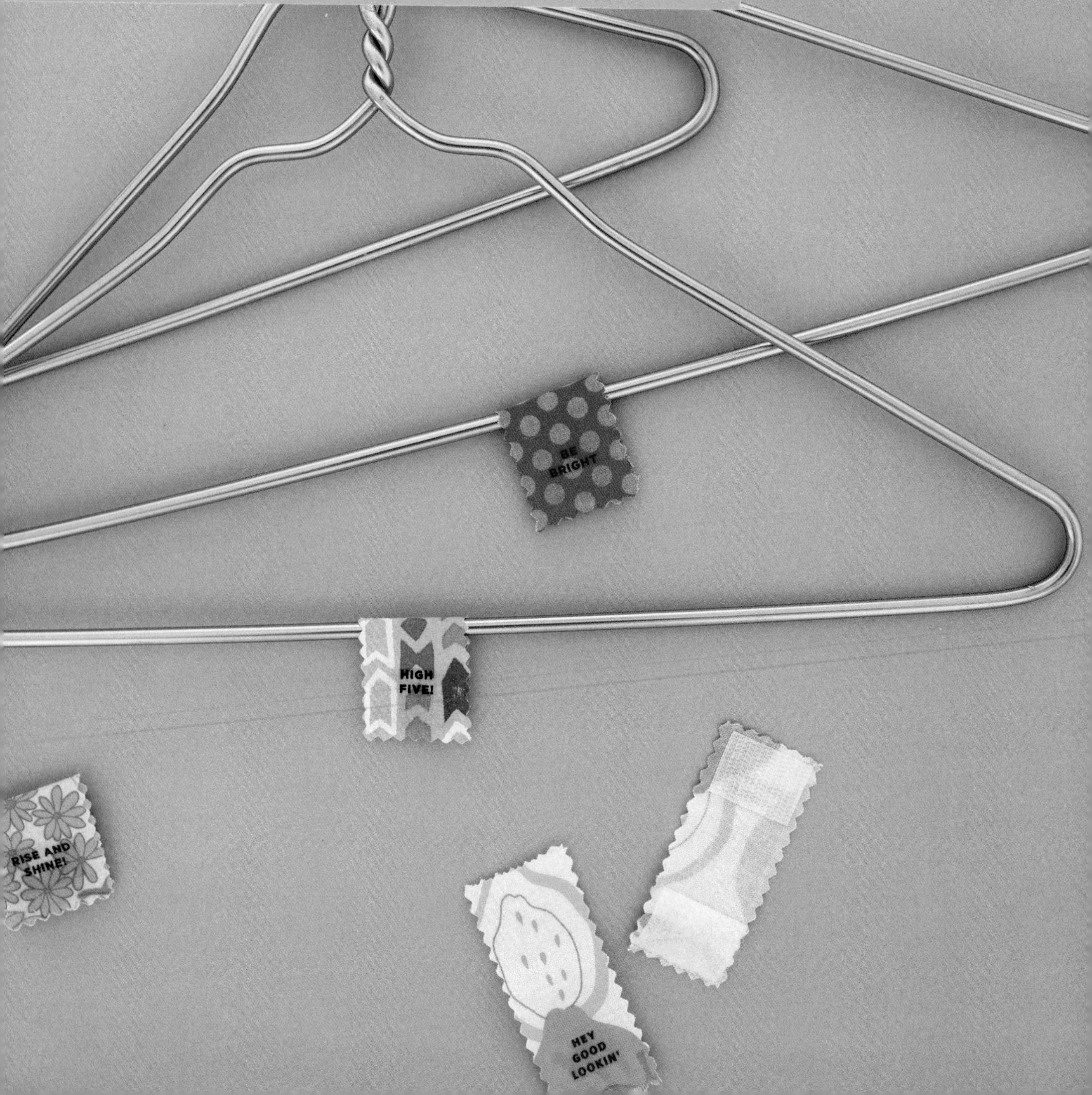

1. Cut a strip of fabric 3 inches long and 1¼ inches wide using scallop fabric shears.

2. Cut Velcro piece 1 x ½-inch square.

3. Iron on Velcro tape to back side of fabric and let cool.

4. Print out templates on iron on transfer sheet.

5. Cut out the templates along the solid line.

6. Iron the words onto fabric. (For specific instructions on transfer time, check your product guidelines.)

7. Once the note is ironed onto the fabric, fold in half and secure Velcro around the hanger.

DRESS IT UP

RISE AND SHINE!

TEMPLATES (PAGE 191)

BE BRIGHT

FUN FABRIC

HEY GOOD LOOKIN'

IRON ON TRANSFER SHEET

SCALLOP FABRIC SHEARS

IRON ON VELCRO

PLASTER POP

PLASTER OF PARIS

1. Decide what word or phrase you want to spell out, the colors you want to use, and then how many you'll need of each letter.

2. Make plaster (use a ratio of 2 parts water to 2 parts plaster of Paris).

3. Mix in drops of tempera paint to make your desired colors (mix in drops of tempera paint to make your desired colors).

4. Pour the mixtures into the tray and let the letters sit for about 20 minutes.

5. Insert a nail into each letter, pointy side out, before the plaster hardens completely (another 18 to 20 minutes. Keep an eye on the plaster—if you insert the nail too late, the plaster will crack).

6. Let the letters sit another 10 minutes after hardening.

7. Remove the letters from the tray and let them sit for 24 hours.

8. To mount the letters to the wall, simply nail small holes into the wall where you plan to place them, then place the letters into the wall.

NAILS
(1¼-INCH WIRE BRADS)

TEMPERA PAINT
(COLORS OF YOUR
CHOICE)

ABC ICE CUBE TRAY

A BLOOMING BACKGROUND

WHETHER YOU'RE LOOKING FOR A QUICK WAY TO LIVEN UP A ROOM OR A BACKDROP FOR A PHOTO-WORTHY CELEBRATION, NOTHING ADDS CHEER QUICKER THAN A WALL OF FLOWERS.

1. Cut 2-inch round circles from contact paper (I love gold!).

2. Test the contact paper on the area ahead of time to make sure it won't harm the wall. Then use the sticky circles to adhere the blooms to the wall.

3. Arrange however you like.

CONTACT PAPER

FLOWERS (PAPER, SILK, OR REAL)

YOU CAN USE PAPER OR SILK FLOWERS FOR
A LONG-TERM DECORATIVE ELEMENT OR LIVE
FLOWERS FOR A SHORT-TERM EVENT.

YOU DON'T HAVE TO BE BETTY CROCKER

I often have this vision of myself—whipping up three-layer cakes from scratch while keeping a toddler wildly entertained, my hair and makeup all intact, and my house perfectly clean. Then I knock myself out of my daydream to the pile of dishes in the sink, a cranky child, and no cake baking in the oven. The reality is that we all do the best we can, and a little creativity can help us make the most of our busy, multitasking lives.

When it comes to making dishes for get-togethers, I am all about sprucing up foods, including desserts that you can buy if you don't have time to make them from scratch. Like our cake toppers, striped cake, or fruity letters, these can all be made using existing foods. Rather than focus on making cookies or cake from scratch, do something with those cookies or that cake that makes them feel special and unique.

MINI NEAPOLITAN CONFETTI CAKES

TINY CAKES ARE MY FAVORITE BECAUSE THEY GIVE YOU JUST THE RIGHT TOUCH OF SWEETNESS IN EACH BITE.

3 SEPARATE SHEET CAKES
(RECIPE PAGE 180)

BUTTER KNIFE

SPRINKLES

SMALL CIRCLE
COOKIE CUTTER
(1- TO 2-INCH DIAMETER)

VANILLA FROSTING
(RECIPE PAGE 182)

1. Make 1 sheet cake in each of the 3 cake flavors (strawberry, confetti, and chocolate) in 9 x 13-inch baking pans. Cool the cakes thoroughly.

2. Use the cookie cutter to cut 24 mini cakes out of each cake sheet.

3. Make mini layer cakes by stacking a chocolate layer, a bit of frosting, a confetti layer, a bit more frosting, and a strawberry layer. Repeat to make 24 little layer cakes.

4. Top each mini cake with frosting and sprinkles.

5. Serve within a few hours of assembly.

CANDY CORDS

1. Wrap a strip of clay around a dowel that's approximately the size of the cord you want to cover until it forms a "C" shape around the cord. Leave enough space that it can be removed.

2. Trim the curved strip into ½- or ¾-inch-wide pieces.

3. Repeat with the number of colors you'd like and to make enough to cover the length of the cord.

4. Bake at 240°F for 30 minutes (or follow the baking instructions for your clay).

5. Let cool to room temperature, then pop the clay into your cord.

ROLLING PIN

¼-INCH DOWEL
(OR LARGER DEPENDING ON THE
SIZE OF YOUR CORD TO COVER)

BAKEABLE MOLDING CLAY
(SUCH AS FIMO) IN THE COLORS
OF YOUR CHOICE

X-ACTO KNIFE

MONOGRAM CORK GIFT BOX

WHETHER YOU'RE GIVING SOMETHING HANDMADE OR STORE-BOUGHT, PLACE IT IN THIS CUSTOM BOX AND IT'S SURE TO BE TREASURED FOR A LONG TIME TO COME.

1. Use our provided letter templates (pages 192–217) and pick the letter you want to make.

2. Trace the letter on a piece of cardboard, making 2 versions: a slightly larger one for the top and a slightly smaller one for the bottom.

3. Cut out a 1½- to 2-inch strip of chip board (this is the depth of the box, so the bigger you make this strip, the deeper the box will be). You will need it to be long enough to wrap around the sides of the letter.

4. Place the smaller letter on a table and hold the chip board parallel to the edge of the letter, flush to the table. Glue the chip board strip around the letter to create the box's bottom structure.

5. Repeat step 4 with the larger (top) letter.

6. Cut out the same 2 letter sizes and the side strip from the cork liner.

7. Remove the adhesive back from the cork liner and cover the top, bottom, and sides of the box with the cork.

8. Trim glitter paper, patterned paper, or wrapping paper to line the inside of the box. We used gold paper to line the inside bottom and top and patterned paper for the sides, but you can customize to make any design you like.

9. Spray-paint the outside of the box with your desired color, using 3 coats of paint. Be sure to let each layer dry thoroughly.

PATTERNED PAPER

CARDBOARD

TEMPLATES

CHIP BOARD

HOT GLUE GUN

X-ACTO KNIFE

UTILITY KNIFE

SPRAY PAINT IN YOUR CHOICE OF COLORS

GOLD GLITTER PAPER

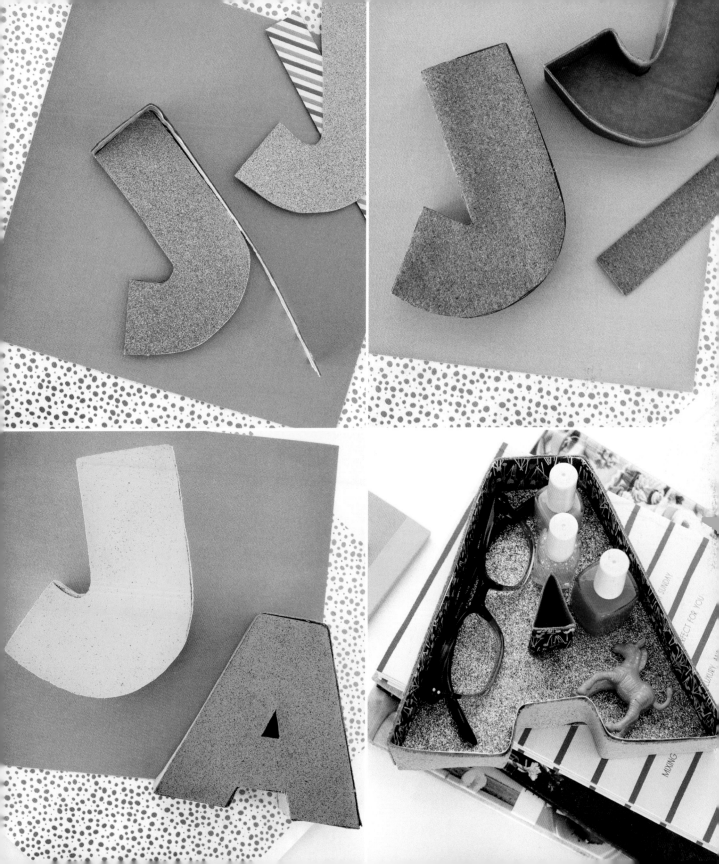

ALPHABET FRUIT

INSPIRED BY ALPHABET SOUP, MAKE A SWEET STATEMENT THAT'S FUN TO EAT WITH THIS FRUIT SALAD.

FIRM FRUIT LIKE CANTELOUPE, COCONUT, AND PINEAPPLE

YAY

1. Slice the fruit into ½-inch-thick pieces.

2. Use cookie cutters to create a mix of letters from the fruit slices.

3. Carefully pop out the cut fruit with a butter knife or skewer.

4. Chill and serve within 24 hours.

MINI ABC COOKIE CUTTERS

YOU CAN ALSO MAKE USE OF THE PIECE LEFT FROM THE CUTOUT BY FILLING IT WITH JELL-O!

BE SILLY

One thing I've learned since becoming a mother is how serious we tend to be as adults. We have so much to worry about and be responsible for, which sometimes hinders our ability to go back to that uninhibited mind-set we had as kids. My daughter, Ruby, reminds me of this every day when she tells me her feet are hiding in the clouds or when she makes a goofy face that turns my stress into a smile.

FLORA-DO

ADD SOME WHIMSY TO YOUR PARTY'S PHOTO BOOTH WITH THIS FLORAL HAIRDO.

1. Cut a piece of Styrofoam that's 1 to 2 feet wide and 1 foot high. You can change the height or width depending on how large you'd like to make your hairdo.

2. Use a wire cutter to trim the stems off the flowers, leaving about ½ inch of stem. This allows you to poke them through the foam without it coming through the back side.

3. Arrange an assortment of silk flowers in the Styrofoam to create the hairdo of your dreams. Be sure to fill the area so no white shows through. Trim the excess Styrofoam when you've filled the area you want.

4. Add ribbon or any additional adornments.

5. Stick the dowel into the base of the foam on one side to use as a handle. Remove it, add hot glue inside the hole, and insert the dowel again. Now you have the perfect photo prop for your next soiree.

RIBBON

SILK FLOWERS

STYROFOAM
(ABOUT 1-INCH THICK)

WIRE CUTTERS

HOT GLUE

DOWEL

A WAY WITH WORDS

How do you say something sweet and simple that makes someone laugh or smile? Everyone's version of the perfect phrase differs. For me, I like phrases that are short and sweet and a little cheeky without being too cutesy. Phrases can be inspired by songs, favorite sayings, or things you actually want to say out loud but might be too afraid to do so.

POP-UP WRAP

CUSTOMIZE A GIFT WITH THE RECIPIENT'S NAME, FAVORITE PHRASE, OR ANY OTHER FUN MESSAGE YOU WANT TO EXPRESS.

HAPPY BIRTH

1. Print out the pop-up ABC templates (page 218).

2. Choose a word or phase of your choice that will fit onto the top of the box you're wrapping.

3. Choose which wrapping paper you want for the outside of the box and which you want to show through the cutouts. (You need a much smaller piece for behind the cutouts and can use leftover scraps, too.)

4. Measure out where the top of the box will be when wrapped in the paper so you know that the area you're cutting will be on the top.

5. Print the letter templates onto regular paper and cut out the letters of your choice— simply cut outside each letter so there is white space around it.

6. Place the first letter into position on your wrapping paper and use an X-Acto knife to cut through both the template and the wrapping paper. Cut along the black line and fold on the orange line to indicate where to fold the wrapping paper.

7. Repeat with the rest of the letters.

8. Cut the inside paper to be large enough to show behind all the cut-out letters. Tape it underneath the top paper layer so the pattern shows through the letters.

9. Wrap the present with the outside layer.

AT LEAST TWO STYLES OF
WRAPPING PAPER

ABC TEMPLATES

SCISSORS

X-ACTO KNIFE AND
CUTTING BOARD

FLORA ON THE GO

MAKE THIS TRAVEL VASE TO GIVE THE GIFT OF A CONSTANT BLOOM.

1. If your toothbrush holder has drainage holes on the bottom, place some caulk inside to cover the holes, then cover the outside bottom with a tiny piece of duct tape that's just wide enough to cover the holes.

2. Spray paint the entire holder with primer. Dry thoroughly.

3. Spray paint the holder in the color of your choice. Dry thoroughly.

4. Create the strap by cutting 2 strips from the faux leather fabric long enough to wrap around the holder like a belt.

5. Iron on a small square piece of Velcro on both strips so as to secure the loops together in the back like a belt or necklace.

6. Fill with a little water and some flowers and hang wherever you please!

FAUX LEATHER

SPRAY PAINT PRIMER

CAULK

SPRAY PAINT
(COLOR OF YOUR CHOICE)

VELCRO

TRAVEL TOOTHBRUSH HOLDER
(THE BOTTOM PIECE)

DUCT TAPE

COOL CONTACT

HERE ARE A FEW OF MY FAVORITE WAYS TO TURN SOMETHING FROM SIMPLE TO AMAZING, JUST WITH CONTACT PAPER. THE BEST PART IS, IT'S EASILY REMOVABLE WHEN YOU WANT TO CHANGE IT UP!

CONTACT PAPER IS ONE OF MY FAVORITE THINGS ON EARTH. I'D MAKE A BOOK OF JUST THINGS TO DO WITH CONTACT PAPER IF I COULD.

SPRUCE IT UP WITH A FRESH
PATTERN OF YOUR CHOICE.

TURN A TYPICALLY UNATTRACTIVE ITEM INTO SOMETHING WITH REAL CHARACTER.

CREATE A MODERN LOOK BY ALTERNATING VARIOUS COLORS TO RUN ALONG THE CENTER OF YOUR DINING TABLE.

ADD AN ACCENT BY DECORATING THE LEGS WITH STRIPES OF CONTACT PAPER.

FANCY FEET

ADD A SPRING TO YOUR STEP WITH THESE EASY-TO-CREATE PATTERNED INSOLES.

IRON-ON FABRIC ADHESIVE

FABRIC OF YOUR CHOICE
(YOU CAN EVEN USE AN OLD SHIRT YOU LOVE)

STORE-BOUGHT INSOLES

1. Use the insole as a pattern to cut out the fabric and iron-on adhesive.

2. Place the adhesive on the insole and top with the fabric. Iron to set as directed by the instructions on the adhesive.

3. Trim the patterned insoles to fit your shoes.

VISIT FUN AND INSPIRING PLACES

It can be easy to sit in front of a computer all day and get stuck in an inspiration rut. I constantly try to stay inspired by getting away from my desk and taking trips to fun and inspiring places around town. They could be museums, the local farmers' market, a vintage bookstore, or even a beautiful candy shop. Any place that's full of color and life is bound to give you a new perspective on things and, at the least, be a new adventure for your day.

CANDY CHARACTERS

MAKE ANY CONFECTION A LITTLE SWEETER WITH THIS CAST OF QUIRKY CHARACTERS.

1. Use our templates (page 220) to draw characters onto the cellophane (or draw your very own cast of characters).

2. Make your very own personalized candy friends by placing candies according to where the head and body would go.

3. Get creative!

SMALL CANDY OF YOUR CHOICE

CANDY WRAPPER CELLOPHANE SQUARES

TEMPLATES

PERMANENT MARKER

STUCK ON YOU

ADD SOME FUN TO YOUR FRIDGE AND CUSTOMIZE YOUR LATEST MEMORIES WITH THESE WHIMSICAL MAGNETS.

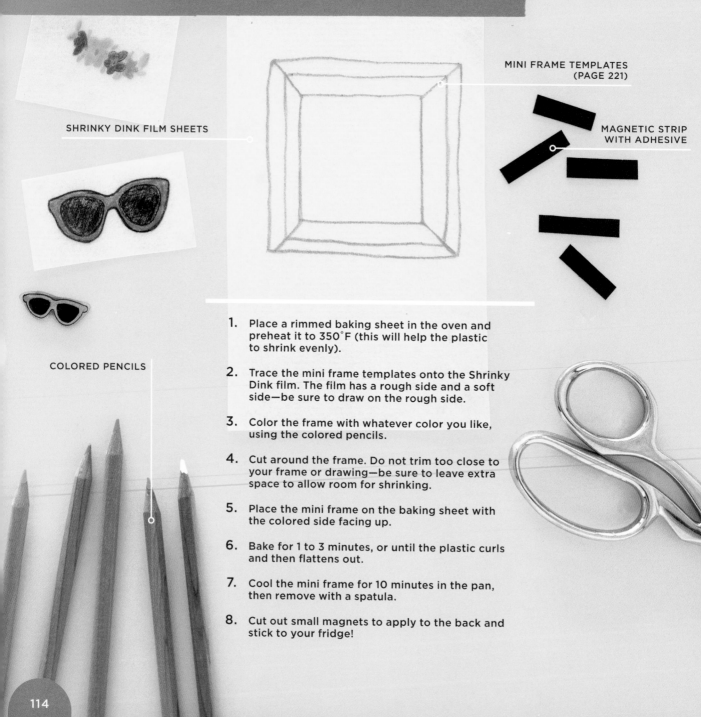

MINI FRAME TEMPLATES (PAGE 221)

SHRINKY DINK FILM SHEETS

MAGNETIC STRIP WITH ADHESIVE

COLORED PENCILS

1. Place a rimmed baking sheet in the oven and preheat it to 350°F (this will help the plastic to shrink evenly).

2. Trace the mini frame templates onto the Shrinky Dink film. The film has a rough side and a soft side—be sure to draw on the rough side.

3. Color the frame with whatever color you like, using the colored pencils.

4. Cut around the frame. Do not trim too close to your frame or drawing—be sure to leave extra space to allow room for shrinking.

5. Place the mini frame on the baking sheet with the colored side facing up.

6. Bake for 1 to 3 minutes, or until the plastic curls and then flattens out.

7. Cool the mini frame for 10 minutes in the pan, then remove with a spatula.

8. Cut out small magnets to apply to the back and stick to your fridge!

PARTY PUFFS

WHETHER YOU'RE MAKING A BACKDROP FOR A PARTY PHOTO BOOTH OR LOOKING FOR A WAY TO DECORATE A ROOM FOR AN EVERYDAY PARTY, THESE SHAPED PUFFS MAKE ANY SPACE MORE WHIMSICAL AND FESTIVE.

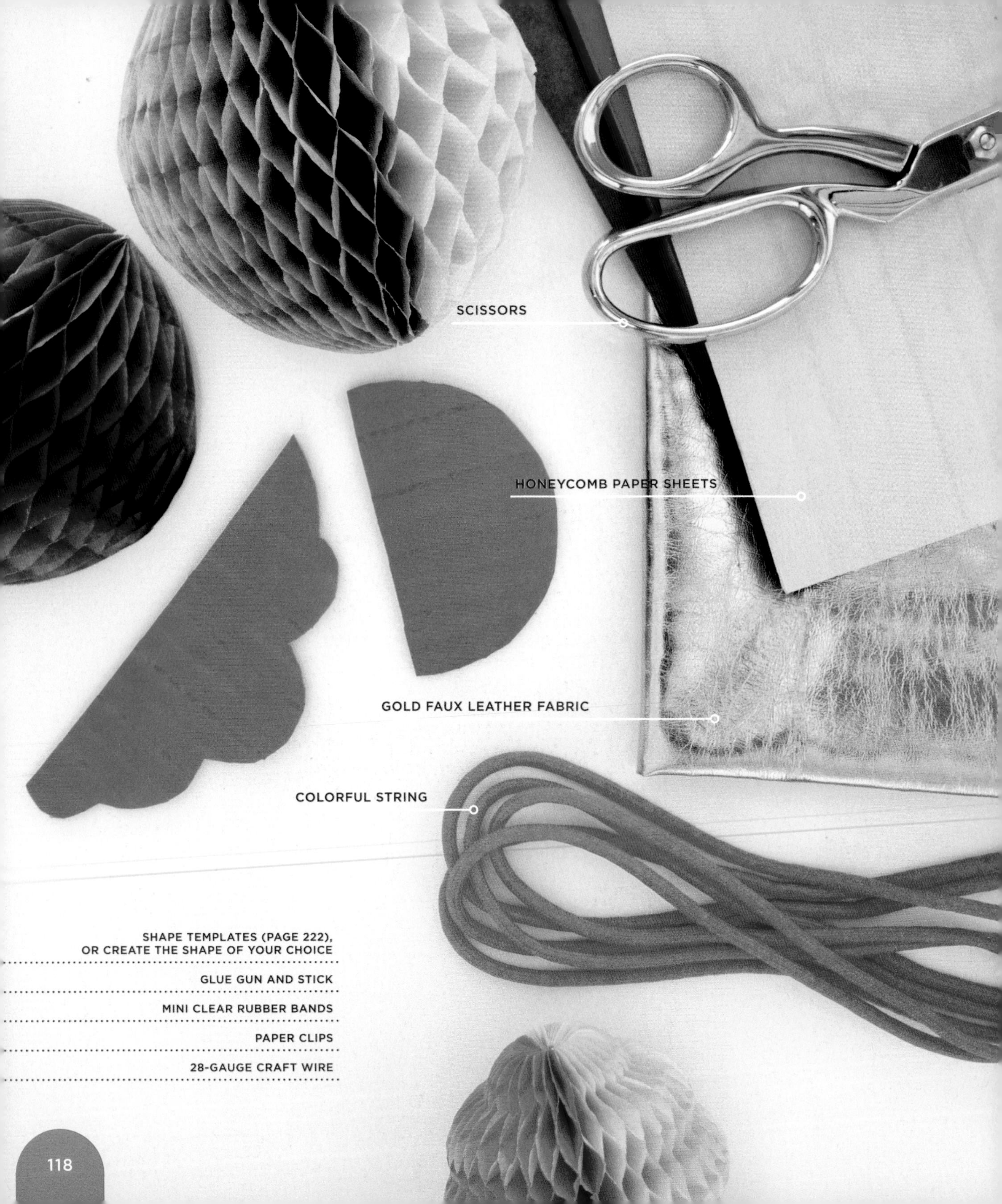

SCISSORS

HONEYCOMB PAPER SHEETS

GOLD FAUX LEATHER FABRIC

COLORFUL STRING

SHAPE TEMPLATES (PAGE 222),
OR CREATE THE SHAPE OF YOUR CHOICE

GLUE GUN AND STICK

MINI CLEAR RUBBER BANDS

PAPER CLIPS

28-GAUGE CRAFT WIRE

1. Trace or photocopy the templates onto the honeycomb paper (or draw your own shapes). To be sure that you will be cutting out the honeycomb on the right side, make sure the lines are horizontal.

2. Choose two colors to block together to make one shape and use a glue stick to glue one side together. Cut a piece of cord about 40 inches long, or as long as you need it for your display. Leaving about 2 inches at the bottom, place the cord along the inside of the honeycomb and secure with hot glue.

3. Make a tassel for the end of each honeycomb string. Cut the gold fabric into ¼-inch strips about 8 inches long. Fold the strips in half with the gold side out and secure with a split ring leaving a tiny loop big enough to add another split ring through. Thread the 2-inch end of the cord through the loop and secure the tassel to the end of the honeycomb.

4. Use a glue stick to glue the remaining side of the honeycomb and open the ball all the way and secure the top and bottom of the honeycomb with paper clips. Add multiple honeycombs to the string as desired—you can place them end to end or leave space between them.

TASTY TOPPINGS

Keep these simple toppings on hand for adding some extra crunch on the fly to your ice cream, yogurt, or cupcake.

Some of my favorite combos:

- **Mini marshmallows and popcorn**
- **An assortment of cereal**
- **Toasted coconut and yogurt drops**
- **Chocolate-dipped sugar cone pieces**
- **Chopped cookies**
- **Dried fruit and nuts**

MINI MARSHMALLOWS
AND POPCORN

CHOCOLATE-DIPPED
SUGAR CONE PIECES

CHOPPED COOKIES

DRIED FRUIT
AND NUTS

TOASTED COCONUT
AND YOGURT DROPS

AN ASSORTMENT
OF CEREAL

ABC TOPPER

BAMBOO SKEWERS

COLORED CARDSTOCK

1. Print out the templates (page 224–229) for
   the letters you want to make.

2. Cut out the letters of your choice along the
   solid lines, then fold them on the dotted lines.

3. Glue the front and back with the skewer in
   the middle.

X-ACTO KNIFE

GLUE STICK OR DOUBLE-SIDED TAPE

SWEET STICKS

FOR A FUN TWIST ON A DESSERT TABLE, OFFER UP SKEWERED SWEETS OF VARIOUS KINDS.

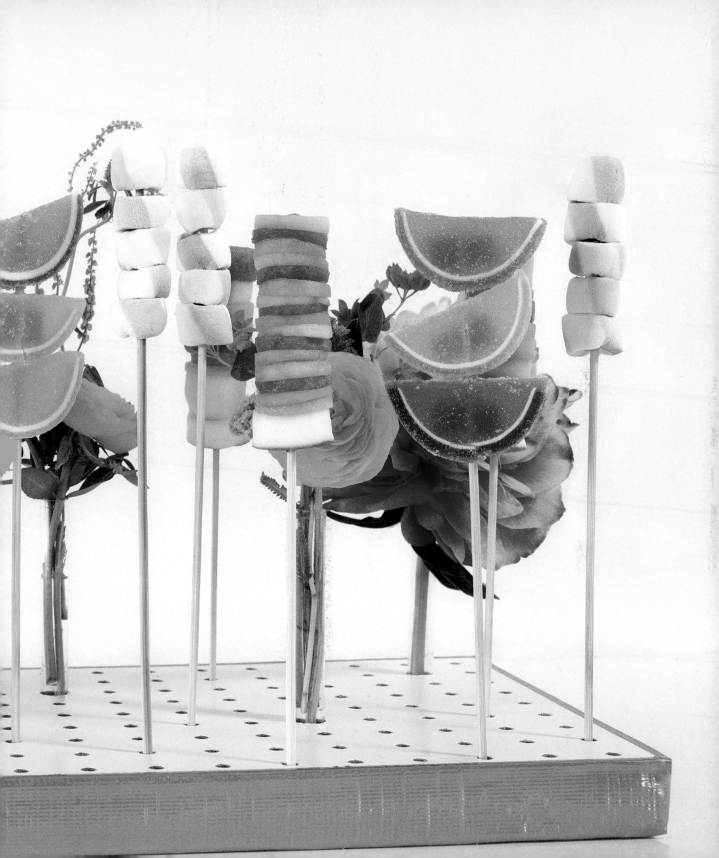

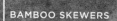

BAMBOO SKEWERS

VARIOUS FRUIT
(MELON WORKS WELL)

SKEWERED SWEETS

1. Cut melon and other fruit into large slices, at least
    1 inch wide and ½ inch thick, then use the cookie
    cutter to cut out small circles.

2. Stack the fruit on sticks as you wish to create
    various striped patterns.

3. Stack gummy and other soft candies on the sticks
    to mix in with the fruit.

4. Insert the skewers into the peg board holes and
    into the Styrofoam base (see pages 128–129).

5. Keep the fruit chilled until ready to serve!

GUMMIES AND OTHER
SOFT CANDIES

TRAY

1. Cut the peg board down to the desired size (this one is 9 x 21 inches).

2. Cut the Styrofoam to the same size as the peg board.

3. If you'd like to add flowers to the display, drill ¼-inch holes in various spots on the board to ½ inch in diameter to hold test tubes.

4. Place the peg board on top of the Styrofoam and line the edge with duct tape. Make sure a bit of the edge overlaps on top to create an even border.

PEG BOARD

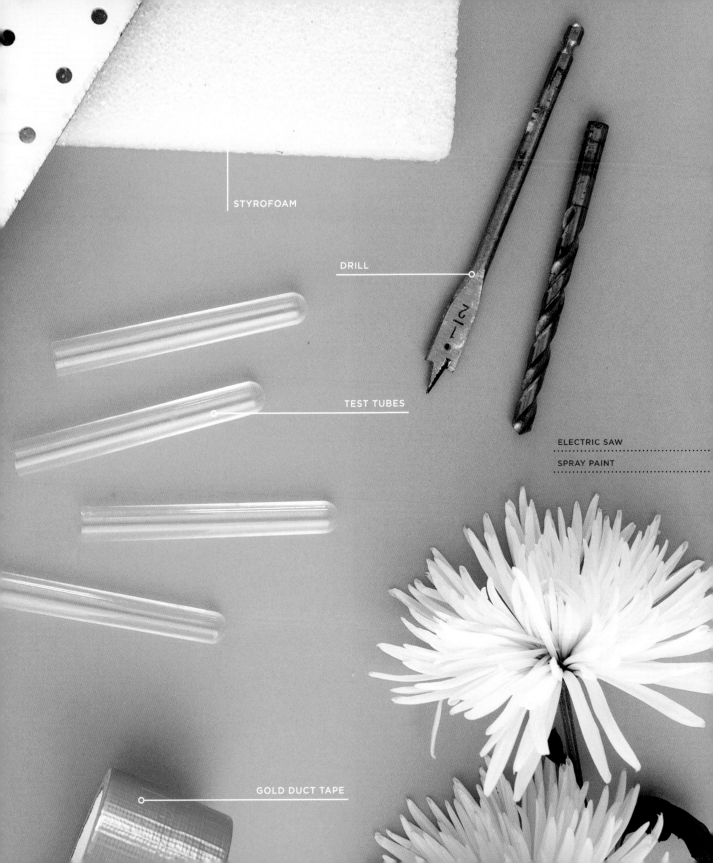

STYROFOAM

DRILL

TEST TUBES

ELECTRIC SAW

SPRAY PAINT

GOLD DUCT TAPE

SURPRISE SCRATCHERS

MAKE YOUR VERY OWN SCRATCH-OFF MESSAGES TO GIVE ANY TIME OF THE YEAR.

1. Print out our templates (page 230) on cardstock, or create your own.

2. Cover the scratch-off side with tape strips placed side by side to cover the whole surface.

3. Mix one part dish soap and two parts acrylic paint.

4. Paint on the scratch-off side.

5. Let dry.

CARDSTOCK

ALL YOU NEED IS
SLEEP.

EAT
DESSERT
FIRST.

SCISSORS OR
X-ACTO KNIFE

PAINT BRUSH

DISH SOAP

CLEAR PACKING TAPE

FORTUNE

NOBODY CAN BE
EXACTLY
LIKE YOU.

ACRYLIC PAINT
(I LIKE GOLD BUT YOU CAN USE
ANY SOLID OR METALLIC COLOR)

LOOK UPSIDE DOWN

Have you ever hung upside down from a tree or a jungle gym? Kids do it all the time, yet we rarely remember to look at our world in new ways and from different angles. When you're stuck in a rut, look at whatever you're doing from a new perspective. It could be as easy as turning the page or project upside down, hanging off the side of your bed while thinking about your problem, or literally taking a different path from your usual route.

TREAT WRAPPERS

MAKE GIFTED COOKIES EVEN MORE SPECIAL BY GIVING THEM THEIR VERY OWN WRAPPER.

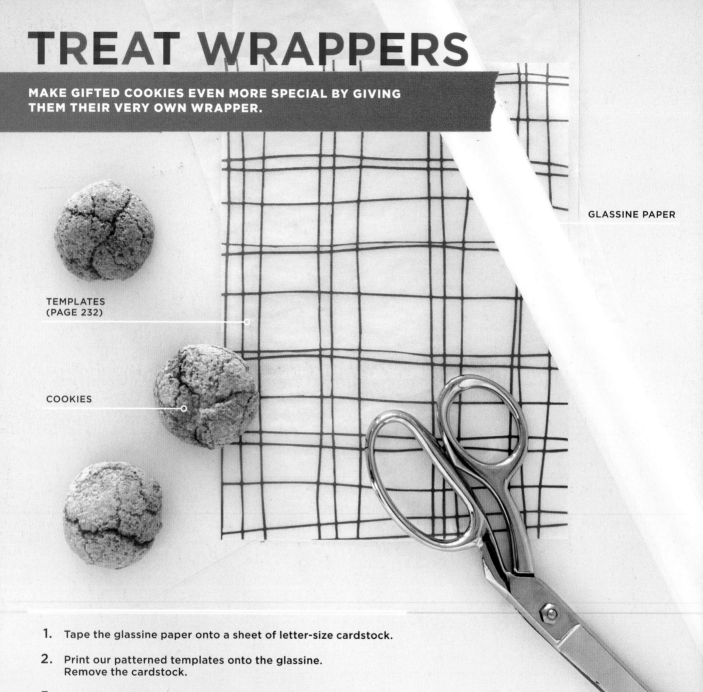

GLASSINE PAPER

TEMPLATES
(PAGE 232)

COOKIES

1. Tape the glassine paper onto a sheet of letter-size cardstock.

2. Print our patterned templates onto the glassine.
   Remove the cardstock.

3. Cut the glassine to size, wrap it around your cookie, and twist
   the ends, as on a piece of candy.

BLOOM IN A BOX

I LOVE JACK-IN-THE-BOXES! HERE'S MY TAKE ON A
CLASSIC WITH BLOOMS THAT WILL LAST A LIFETIME.

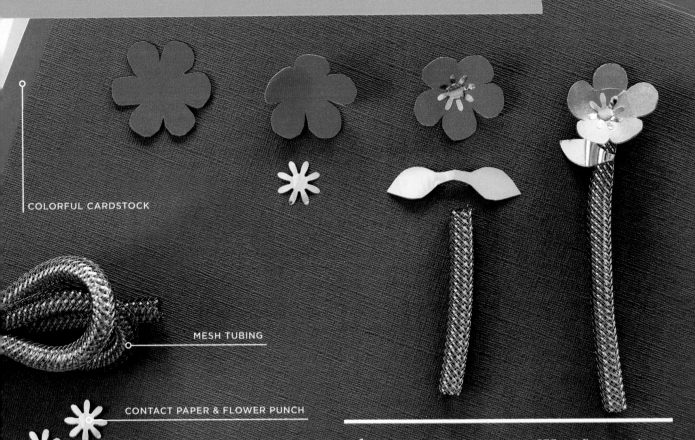

COLORFUL CARDSTOCK

MESH TUBING

CONTACT PAPER & FLOWER PUNCH

SMALL GIFT BOX OR WOODEN BOX,
PREFERABLY WITH A HINGED LID

SUPERGLUE

1. Using the templates on page 237, cut flowers out of cardstock.

2. Punch out the centers of the flowers from contact paper.

3. Glue the centers into the flowers.

4. Cut the mesh into stems of your desired length.

5. Cut cardstock to fit the inside of the box. Punch holes where you would like the flowers to be placed.

6. Cut out leaves from contact paper and glue them onto the stems.

7. Place the flowers within the holes of the cardstock till you've filled it to the desired amount.

GROUPING THINGS IN CLUSTERS

One of my favorite tricks is to take multiples of one simple thing—such as pillows, vases, lamps, or even paper umbrellas—and group them together in various colors in a cluster. The basic piece feels more lush and sophisticated when used in a grouping, and it allows you to instantly add color to something as plain as a white cake and foam core background.

OMBRÉ FRUIT VASES

MAKE USE OF THE BEAUTIFUL EXTERIORS OF YOUR FAVORITE FRUITS BY FILLING THEM WITH FLOWERS FOR YOUR NEXT PARTY.

SHARP KNIFE FOR CARVING

PRIMER (MIGHT BE NEEDED ON SOME
FRUIT FOR THE PAINT TO STICK)

THREE SPRAY PAINT
COLORS PER VASE
(LIGHT/MEDIUM/DARK
VERSIONS OF A SINGLE
COLOR WORK BEST)

FRUIT (OR VEGETABLE) WITH A HARD EXTERIOR THAT CAN
BE CARVED OUT ON THE INSIDE (SUCH AS CANTALOUPE,
PINEAPPLE, OR ACORN SQUASH)

1. Spray-paint the entire fruit the lightest color.

2. Spray the bottom half with the middle color, then the bottom third with the darkest color. (You can choose how much of each color you want to use to create your ombré look.)

3. Let dry for a few hours (some spray paints dry more quickly than others).

FLORAL FOAM

4. Cut off the top of the fruit and hollow out the middle.

5. Cut a floral foam brick to fit inside the hollowed-out fruit.

6. Remove the foam from the fruit and float it in a bowl of water with the holey side down until the foam is completely saturated. Do not force the foam underwater. The foam is ready to use when it floats at water level. Return the foam to the fruit's interior.

7. Start the arrangement by putting your main/focal-point flower in the center. Arrange smaller flowers around the main flower until you're happy with the result.

SURPRISE CONFETTI COOKIE

ADD A TWIST TO A SANDWICH COOKIE WITH A COLORFUL SPRINKLED SURPRISE INSIDE.

1. Bake the cookies and let them cool.

2. Pipe a thin circle of icing approximately ¼ inch from the edge of half of the cookies.

3. Let the icing harden slightly, about 5 minutes, then pipe another ring of icing on top of the first which creates a little "house" for your sprinkles.

4. Fill the cookie centers with your desired sprinkles and pipe a third icing ring around the top.

5. While the icing is wet on each cookie, immediately top with a second cookie and press lightly to secure.

6. Let the icing set. Serve within 24 hours.

CHOCOLATE/VANILLA WAFER COOKIES (RECIPE PAGE 185)

SPRINKLES (MIX A FEW KINDS TOGETHER!)

ROYAL ICING (RECIPE PAGE 184)

144

BUYING VINTAGE CLOTHING

I'm a big fan of mixing vintage clothing in with my everyday wardrobe, as I love having unique pieces that not everyone has. But it can be super intimidating to walk into a vintage store with racks and racks of often random and mixed merchandise and finding those diamonds in the rough.

Here are some tips on buying vintage clothing:

1. Go into it knowing what cuts fit you the best. Do you prefer flowy dresses or very tailored ones? Do you like knee-length or ankle-length skirts? Do you prefer shirts with a boatneck or a crew neck? If you have a general idea of what's most flattering on your body type before going, you're more likely to be able to quickly edit through pieces you find and spend less time convincing yourself to buy a garment that's not flattering at all, simply because you like the floral fabric it's made of.

2. Go in with a general mission. What would you be really happy walking away with? A dress, a skirt, or a few great scarves?

3. Keeping these thoughts in mind, let your eyes and hands do the wandering. With racks and racks of clothing, you'll have to decipher initially by the colors or patterns that you see. Pull out pieces to examine further, as you would with any other shopping experience, but be quicker to put back anything that doesn't have the right fit for you, that has visible stains or tears, or that just turns out to be less special than it seemed from afar.

4. Once you're trying on some possible options, remember that you can alter vintage clothing to make it fit even better. I often shorten the hem on a dress, bring in a skirt at the waist, or turn a long-sleeve top into a short-sleeve one. You don't want to change it completely, but if the piece has a great structure that just needs a bit of altering, then it's a great way to make it fit you perfectly and get the unique quality of the vintage item all at once.

BROOCH THE SUBJECT

ONE OF MY FAVORITE ACCESSORIES TO ADD TO ANY OUTFIT IS A PRETTY VINTAGE BROOCH. MAKE YOUR OWN BY COMBINING AN ASSORTMENT OF FOUND GOODIES.

1. Choose pieces from your vintage finds that will fit onto the square glass tile. Set them into place as desired.

2. Use craft adhesive to glue the pieces onto the tile. Dry about 10 minutes, then glue on the backing pin. Dry another 10 minutes.

3. Use superglue to glue the brooch backing pin to the back of the tile. Dry thoroughly.

VINTAGE FINDS
(SUCH AS LETTERS, BEADS,
AND SO ON)

20MM GOLD RHINESTONE
CHUNKY BEAD

⅞-INCH INCH SQUARE
CLEAR GLASS JEWELRY
PENDANT TILES

E6000 PERMANENT
CRAFT ADHESIVE

SUPERGLUE

BROOCH BACKING PINS

PLASTIC ANIMAL,
SPRAY PAINTED

FARMERS' MARKET BAG

MAKE YOUR VERY OWN MARKET BAG FOR TOTING AROUND YOUR WEEKLY HARVEST.

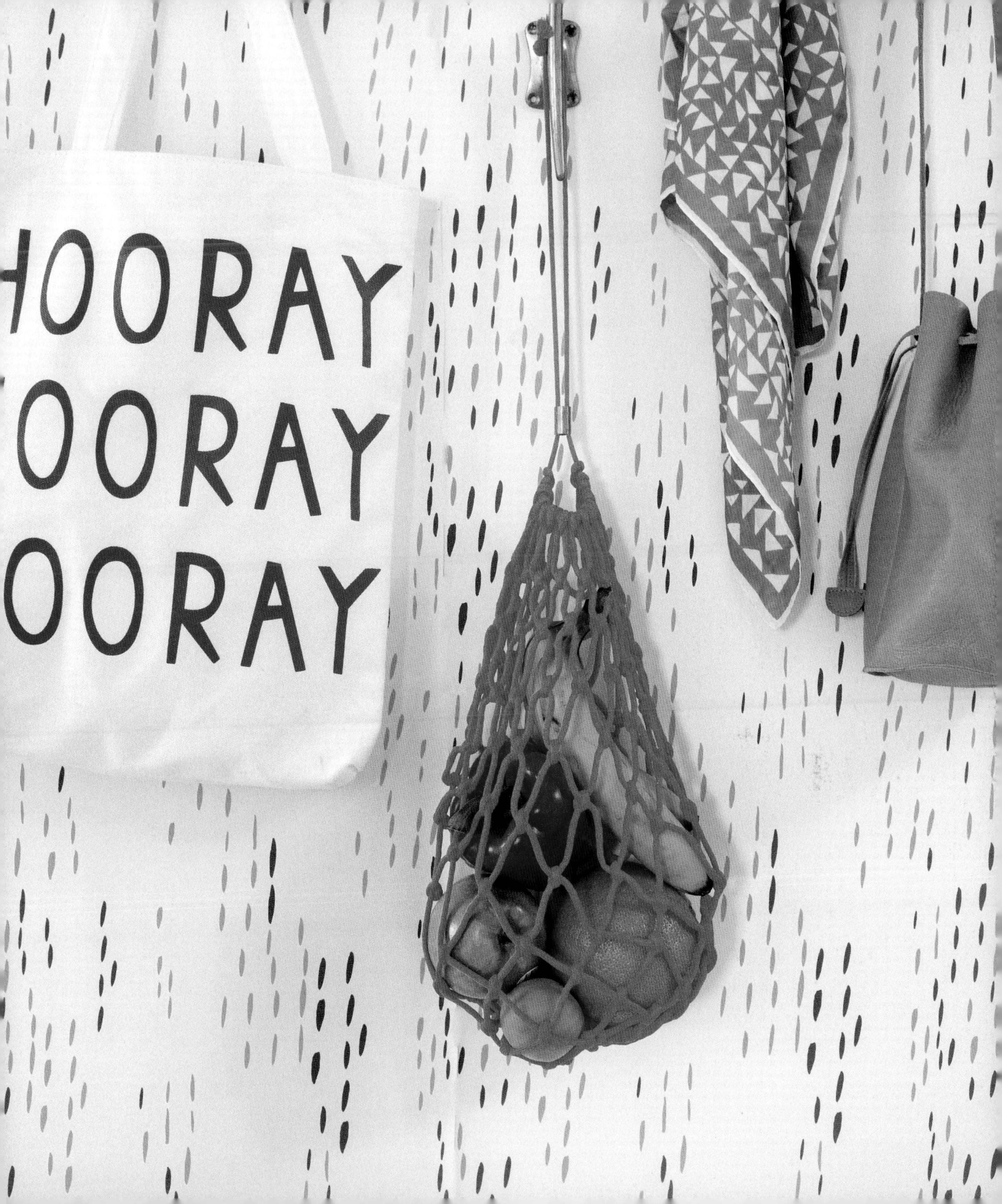
HOORAY
OORAY
OORAY

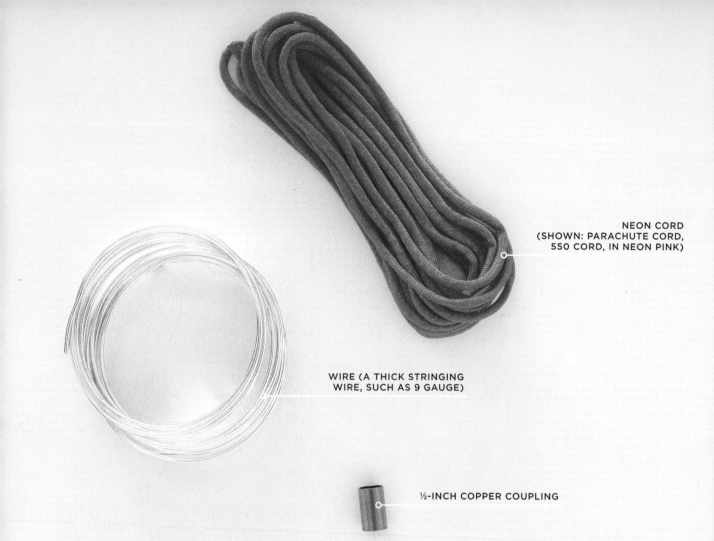

NEON CORD
(SHOWN: PARACHUTE CORD,
550 CORD, IN NEON PINK)

WIRE (A THICK STRINGING
WIRE, SUCH AS 9 GAUGE)

½-INCH COPPER COUPLING

1. Make an 8-inch circle with the stringing wire (create little hooks on each end and clasp them together).

2. The length of the strands of rope you use will determine the size bag you get. Cut an 80-inch piece of cord and wrap it around the wire circle. Secure the end by tying it into a knot. This will be your drawstring.

3. Cut 15 pieces of 60-inch cord.

4. Wrap each piece of rope onto the circle wire, going all the way around. Once all pieces of rope are on the circle wire, take 2 cords and tie them into a knot. Work around the circle to tie the rest of the cords.

5. To secure the end, tie the loose strands together by cutting another piece of cord and wrapping it around tightly and tying a double knot. Cut any longer loose strands.

6. Carefully remove the circle wire, taking care not to cut the cord that you wrapped around the wire.

7. Untie the knot at the top and put in the copper coupling, which will now serve as a drawstring. Tie the end of the rope at the top into a secure knot.

8. Turn the bag inside out so that the end of the bag with the excess rope is on the inside.

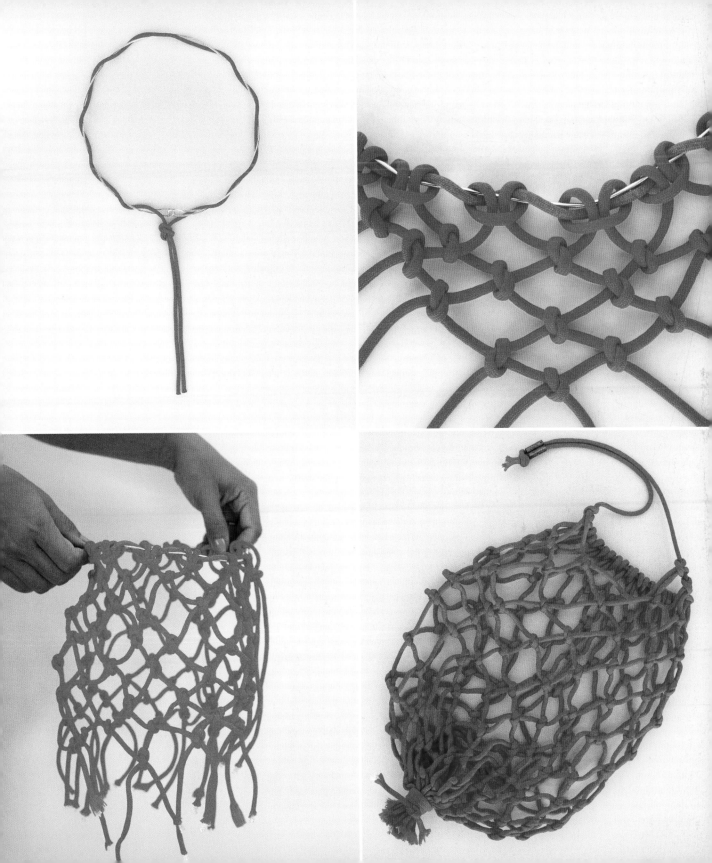

MY FAVORITE FLOWERS

I love flowers and find it to such a treat to pick up a bunch from the farmers' market or grocery store on a weekly basis to keep on my desk or dining table, as they bring life, literally, to any room. Here are a few of my favorite go-to flowers (and a couple of other fun things) to add to an arrangement to make for yourself or as a gift:

- **Kumquats:** If you have access to a kumquat tree, these are so fun to add to a cluster of flowers for their contrast in shape and color, and they're edible!

- **Dusty miller:** Especially for wintry bouquets, dusty millers add some extra foliage and texture to your flowers.

- **Lisianthus:** Soft and organic, these are a great flower to incorporate instead of roses for a more wildflower look.

- **Craspedia:** Part of the daisy family, these whimsical flowers add color and fun to any arrangement.

- **Dahlias:** Dahlias come in a range of sizes, colors, and shapes and are a beautiful flower to use as the focal point of a bunch of blooms.

- **Freesia:** Beautiful as a single stem or grouped with others, freesias are delightful on the nose as well as the eyes.

- **Mint:** Although it's not a flower, I love adding a sprig of mint to a centerpiece. It smells so refreshing and adds instant texture.

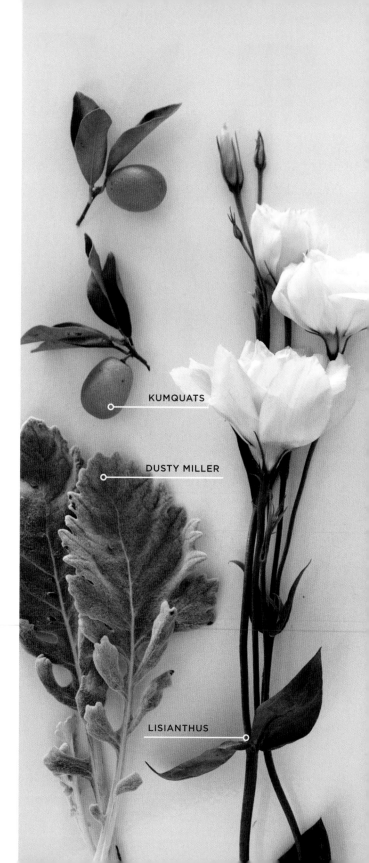

KUMQUATS

DUSTY MILLER

LISIANTHUS

CRASPEDIA

FREESIA

DAHLIA

DAHLIA

MINT

PUFF VASES

MAKE USE OF OLD CUPS, GLASSES, AND JARS BY GIVING THEM NEW LIFE AS FUN, TEXTURAL VASES.

1. Wash and dry the glass thoroughly.

2. Place the foam shapes or letters on the glass wherever you like. You can make a pattern or word or shape.

3. Paint the whole cup with 1 coat of primer. Dry thoroughly.

4. Paint the whole cup with 1 coat of spray paint. Dry thoroughly.

5. Finally, if you'd like extra durability, use a non-yellowing clear gloss spray paint top coat.

FOAM LETTERS AND SHAPES (OR A FOAM SHEET WITH AN ADHESIVE BACK SO YOU CAN CUT OUT YOUR OWN SHAPES)

ANY GLASS, MUG, OR CUP THAT YOU NO LONGER NEED

PRIMER

SPRAY PAINT

SPRAY GLOSS TOP COAT (OPTIONAL)

A MINI FEAST

CREATE YOUR VERY OWN HORS D'OEUVRE DISPLAY PIECE FOR EASY ENTERTAINING ANY TIME SOMEONE STOPS BY.

PLEXIGLAS

1. Add strips of contact paper to the bottom of the tea tins.

2. Arrange the tea tins in a horizontal pattern (or whatever shape you prefer).

3. Place them on colorful Plexi to create a base.

4. Fill with a mix of handheld foods and flowers for decoration.

CONTACT PAPER

2-AND 4-OUNCE TEA

FLOWERS (PAPER, SILK, OR REAL)

INSPIRATION VACATION

For many people, a vacation is meant to be a break from everyday life and a time to shut your brain off. For me, it's the opposite. While I do enjoy taking a break from my daily routine and giving my brain a rest, I look at vacations as a time to get inspired by new surroundings. Whether it's to a tropical island, a small desert town, or a countryside in another country, a trip will make you come back brimming with ideas. Take lots of photos, note how the place is different from where you live and where else you've traveled, and bring your ideas home for a new dose of inspiration.

SOURCES

ART & CRAFT SUPPLIES

AARON BROTHERS
AARONBROTHERS.COM
(framing supplies; frames)

CONTAINER STORE
CONTAINERSTORE.COM
(organizational storage supplies;
mailer tubes)

DICK BLICK
DICKBLICK.COM
(art supplies; paint, foam core,
paper, glue, glassine paper)

JOANN FABRICS
JOANN.COM
(craft supplies; fabric, beads,
glue, paper, paint, silk flowers)

MICHAELS
MICHAELS.COM
(craft supplies; glue, beads,
paper, paint, silk flowers, circle
cutter)

MOSKATELS
(art and craft supplies; glue,
beads, paint, paper, silk flowers)

OFFICE DEPOT
OFFICEDEPOT.COM
(office supplies; sticky labels)

PAPER SOURCE
PAPER-SOURCE.COM
(paper, paper cutting supplies)

SANNA ANNUKKA
SANNA-ANNUKKA.COM
(textile design; decorative paper,
wrapping paper)

HARDWARE SUPPLIES

HOME DEPOT
HOMEDEPOT.COM
(hardware supplies; brass screw
nuts, wood, nails)

LOWES
LOWES.COM
(hardware supplies; wood, nails,
metal key ring, steel wire)

TAP PLASTIC
TAPPLASTICS.COM
(unique plastic products;
Plexiglas)

HOME DECOR

ANTHROPOLOGIE
ANTHROPOLOGIE.COM
(clothing and home furnishings; vases, dishes, glassware, napkins, table runners)

A SUNNY AFTERNOON
ASUNNYAFTERNOON.COM
(table top goods; napkins, table runners)

BLOOMS IN THE AIR
BLOOMSINTHEAIR.COM
(decorative paper products; handmade paper flowers)

CB2
CB2.COM
(modern home furnishings; decorative throw pillows)

DESIGN YOUR WALL
DESIGNYOURWALL.COM
(wall decor products; contact paper)

FERM LIVING
FERMLIVING.COM
(Danish home decor; decorative throw pillows)

HOLD N STORAGE
HOLDNSTORAGE.COM
(home storage organization; gold hangers)

JAM PAPER
(office supplies; gold push pins)

JUJU WALLPAPERS
JUJUPAPERS.COM
(hand printed wallpaper; wallpaper)

MOOD FABRIC
MOODFABRICS.COM
(designer fabric and supplies; fabric)

POTTOK
POTTOKPRINTS.COM
(wallpaper studio; wallpaper)

TARGET
TARGET.COM
(home decor items, office supplies, tabletop goods)

TWIG AND TWINE
TWIGANDTWINEDESIGN.COM
(flowers and unique gifts; flowers)

URBANIC
URBANICPAPER.COM
(stationery supplies; decorative papers, greeting cards)

VINTAGE SHOPS

AMERICAN ARCHIVE
ETSY.COM/SHOP/ AMERICANARCHIVE
(vintage apparel)

EBAY
EBAY.COM
(vintage table top and decor)

NICK METROPOLIS
NICKMETROPOLIS.COM
(collectible furniture and decor)

ONE KINGS LANE
ONEKINGSLANE.COM
(vintage decor; vases, figurines, glassware)

SALVAGE LIFE
SALVAGELIFE.COM/
(vintage apparel)

SHAREEN VINTAGE
SHAREEN.COM
(vintage apparel)

EDIBLES

GLORIA'S
GLORIASCAKECANDYSUPLYS.COM
(baking supplies; cellophane
candy wrapper, cookie cutters)

SOCKERBIT
SOCKERBIT.COM
(Scandinavian candy store;
candy)

STRAND TEA
STRANDTEA.COM
(tea supplies; tea tins)

SURFAS
CULINARYDISTRICT.COM
(baking supplies; candy, spices,
cookie cutters)

SUR LA TABLE
SURLATABLE.COM
(kitchen supplies; marble pastry
board)

SWEET FACTORY
SWEETFACTORY.COM
(candy store; bulk candy)

SPECIALTY ITEMS

32 DEGREES NORTH
VINTAGE-ORNAMENTS.COM
(craft supplies; honeycombs)

AMAZON
AMAZON.COM
(various specialty items; neon
EL wire, Plexiglas box, cocktail
umbrellas, test tubes, silicone
ABC baking mold)

BUDDY BELLE SUPPLIES
ETSY.COM/SHOP/
BUDDYBELLESUPPLIES
(craft supplies; chunky rhinestone
beads)

LULUS CUPCAKE BOUTIQUE
ETSY.COM/SHOP/
LULUSCUPCAKEBOUTIQUE
(decorative baking supplies; mini
figurines and cake toppers)

THE HEY DAY SHOP
ETSY.COM/SHOP/
THEHEYDAYSHOP
(decorative fabric supplies; gold
faux fabric)

TRAIN SHACK
TRAINSHACK.COM
(toy train accessories and
supplies; grass and tulips)

RECIPES

STRIPED OMBRÉ CAKE

Makes one 8-inch round cake

3 large eggs, separated

⅓ cup sugar

1 tablespoon honey

½ cup all-purpose flour

1 tablespoon plus 1 teaspoon milk

Preheat the oven to 325°F. Prepare an 8-inch cake pan by greasing the sides and lining the bottom with parchment paper.

With a hand or stand mixer, whisk egg whites on medium-low until frothy, about 2 minutes. Turn mixer to medium-high and gradually add sugar, whisking until firm peaks form.

With the speed on low, add the yolks one at a time, until incorporated.

Add the honey and whisk on low until just combined.

Sift the flour onto the egg mixture and fold it in with a rubber spatula until just combined.

Drizzle the milk on top of the batter and fold in until just combined.

Pour the batter into the prepared pan. Gently tap the pan on the countertop 3 or 4 times to remove large air bubbles.

Bake for 28 to 30 minutes, or until the top is evenly browned.

Immediately run a thin metal spatula or knife around the pan to loosen the cake. Let cool for 2 to 3 minutes, then invert on cooling rack.

MINI NEAPOLITAN CONFETTI CAKES

Strawberry Cake
Confetti Cake
Chocolate Cake
Vanilla Frosting

Strawberry Cake

½ cup milk

1 teaspoon white vinegar

½ cup strawberry puree (made from about 1 cup whole fresh or frozen strawberries)

2 tablespoons plus ⅓ cup sugar

1¼ cups all-purpose flour

2 tablespoons cornstarch

¾ teaspoon baking powder

½ teaspoon baking soda

¼ teaspoon salt

⅓ cup vegetable oil

1 teaspoon pure vanilla extract

2 drops natural red food coloring (optional for a brighter pink color)

Preheat the oven to 350°F. Grease and flour a 9 x 13-inch baking pan.

In a small bowl, whisk the milk and vinegar and set aside. The mixture will curdle.

In a small saucepan over low heat, simmer the strawberry puree and 2 tablespoons sugar until the mixture is slightly reduced and thickened, about 5 minutes. Remove from the heat and set aside.

Into a medium bowl, sift together the flour, cornstarch, baking powder, baking soda, and salt.

In a large bowl, beat the milk mixture, strawberry puree, oil, remaining ⅓ cup sugar, vanilla extract, and food coloring, if using. Add the dry mixture and whisk just until no lumps remain.

Pour the batter into the prepared baking pan and bake for 20 to 25 minutes, or until a skewer comes out clean. Let cool.

Confetti Cake

1 cup milk

1 teaspoon white vinegar

1¼ cups all-purpose flour

2 tablespoons cornstarch

½ teaspoon baking powder

½ teaspoon baking soda

¼ teaspoon salt

⅓ cup vegetable oil

¾ cup sugar

2 teaspoons pure vanilla extract

⅓ cup sprinkles

Preheat the oven to 350°F. Grease and flour a 9 x 13-inch baking pan and set aside.

In a small bowl, whisk the milk and vinegar and set aside. The mixture will curdle.

In a medium bowl, sift the flour, cornstarch, baking powder, baking soda, and salt.

In a large bowl, beat the milk mixture, oil, sugar, and vanilla extract. Add the dry mixture and whisk just until no lumps remain. Fold in the sprinkles.

Pour the batter into the prepared pan and bake for 20 to 25 minutes, or until a skewer comes out clean. Let cool.

Chocolate Cake

1⅓ cups milk

1 teaspoon white vinegar

1 cup all-purpose flour

⅓ cup cocoa powder

½ teaspoon baking powder

1 teaspoon baking soda

¼ teaspoon salt

½ cup vegetable oil

¾ cup sugar

1 tablespoon pure vanilla extract

Preheat the oven to 350°F. Grease and flour a 9 x 13-inch baking pan and set aside.

In a small bowl, whisk the milk and vinegar and set aside. The mixture will curdle.

In a medium bowl, sift the flour, cocoa powder, baking powder, baking soda, and salt.

In a large bowl, beat the milk mixture, oil, sugar, and vanilla extract. Add the dry mixture and whisk just until no lumps remain.

Pour the batter into the prepared pan and bake for 20 to 25 minutes, or until a skewer comes out clean. Let cool.

Vanilla Frosting

1 stick (½ cup/4 ounces) butter, at room temperature

1 cup powdered sugar

1 tablespoon milk

1 teaspoon pure vanilla extract

With a hand or stand mixer, beat the butter on medium speed until pale and smooth, about 5 minutes.

Add the powdered sugar, milk, and vanilla and beat on low until combined. Turn the mixer to medium speed and beat until very light and fluffy. Use immediately.

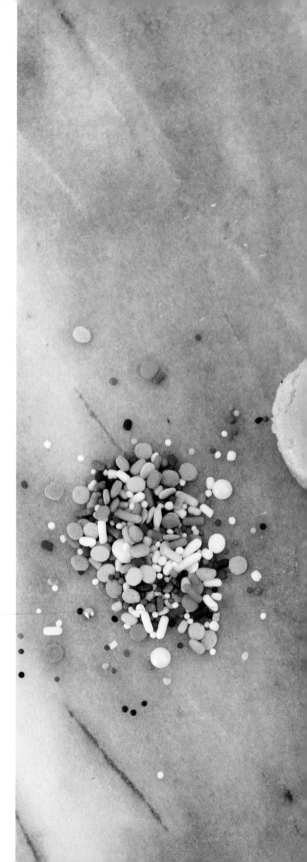

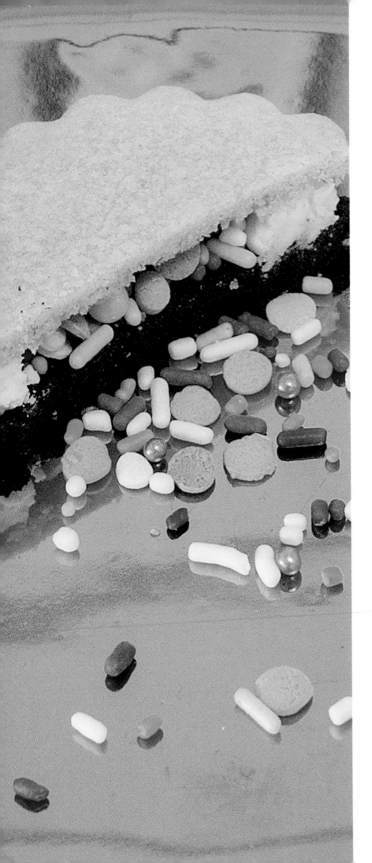

SURPRISE CONFETTI COOKIE

Makes one 8-inch round cake

Royal Icing Crisp Chocolate Cookies Vanilla Cookies

Crisp Chocolate Cookies

1½ cups all-purpose flour

½ cup Dutch process cocoa

1 teaspoon baking powder

¼ teaspoon salt

1 stick (½ cup) unsalted butter, at room temperature

¾ cup sugar

1 large egg

1 teaspoon pure vanilla extract

Into a medium bowl, sift together the flour, cocoa, baking powder, and salt.

Using a stand or hand mixer on medium speed, beat the butter and sugar until light and fluffy, about 3 minutes. Add the egg and vanilla and continue to beat until fully combined.

Switching to the lowest speed, gradually add the dry ingredients to the butter mixture until a soft dough forms. Remove the dough from the bowl and wrap it tightly in plastic wrap. Refrigerate the dough for 30 minutes to 1 hour.

When you're ready to bake the cookies, preheat the oven to 350°F and line a baking sheet with parchment paper.

Divide the dough into 4 portions. Roll one portion of the dough between 2 sheets of parchment paper to ¼- to ⅛-inch thickness.

Cut the dough into the desired shape and place on the baking sheet. Bake for 8 to 10 minutes, or until lightly crisped. Let the cookies cool slightly on the baking sheet before transferring them to a cooling rack.

Vanilla Cookies

2 cups all-purpose flour

½ teaspoon baking powder

½ teaspoon baking soda

½ teaspoon salt

1 stick (½ cup/4 ounces) butter

1 cup sugar

1 large egg

1 teaspoon pure vanilla extract

Into a medium bowl, sift the flour, baking powder, baking soda, and salt.

Using a stand or hand mixer on medium speed, beat the butter and sugar until light and fluffy, about 3 minutes. Add the egg and vanilla extract and continue to beat until fully combined.

Switching to the lowest speed, gradually add the dry ingredients to the butter mixture until a soft dough forms. Wrap the dough tightly in plastic wrap, and refrigerate for 30 minutes to 1 hour.

When you're ready to bake the cookies, preheat the oven to 350°F and line a baking sheet with parchment paper. Divide the dough into 4 portions. Roll one portion at a time between 2 sheets of parchment paper to ¼- to ⅛-inch thickness.

Cut dough into the desired shape and place on the baking sheet. Bake for 8 to 10 minutes, or until lightly crisp. Let the cookies cool slightly on the baking sheet before transferring them to a cooling rack.

Royal Icing

1 large egg white

1 teaspoon pure vanilla extract

2 cups confectioners' sugar

Using a hand or stand mixer, whisk the egg white and vanilla until frothy. Gradually add the sugar and mix on low until smooth. Turn the mixer to medium-high and whisk until the mixture forms stiff, glossy peaks, about 7 minutes.

Transfer to piping bag immediately and twist the top closed to remove any exposure to air (you don't want it to firm up before it's piped).

TEMPLATES

You can find all of the printable templates for the Oh Joy! projects in this book in the following pages. Simply copy the pages at 100 percent.

You can download PDF files of these templates at ohjoy.com/booktemplates.

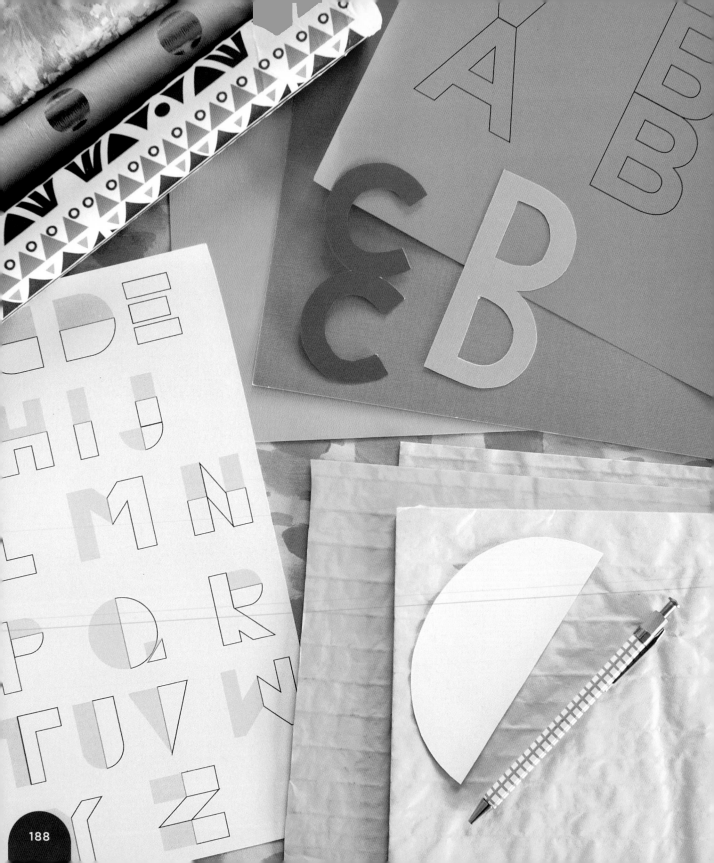

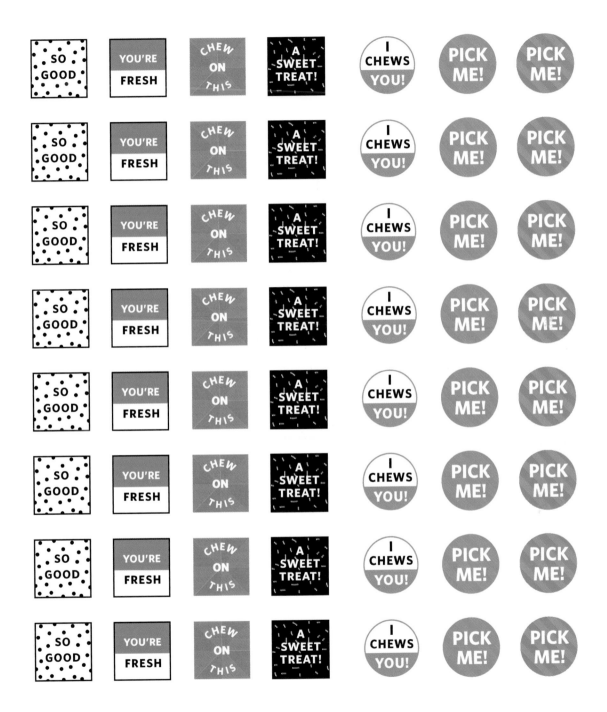

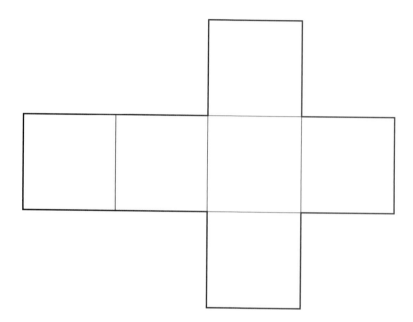

HIGH
FIVE!

HEY
GOOD
LOOKIN',

GOOD
MORNING!

DRESS
IT UP

RISE AND
SHINE!

BE
BRIGHT

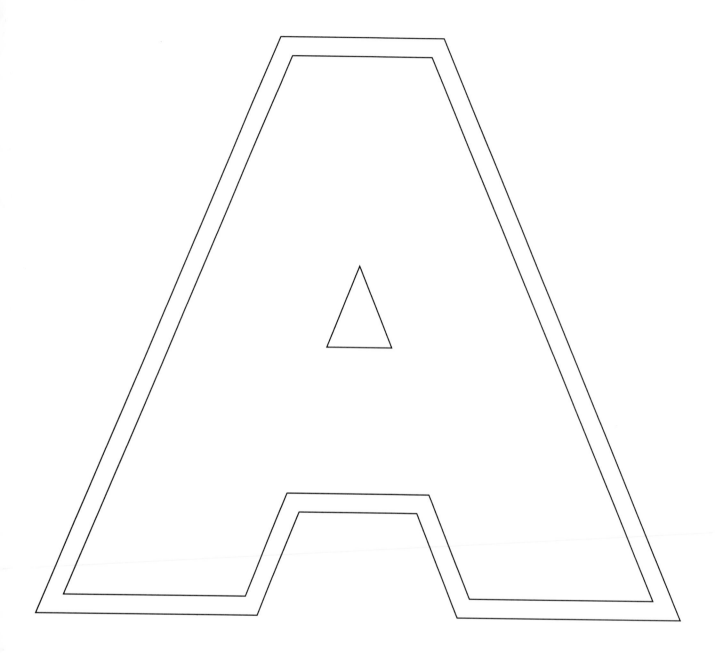

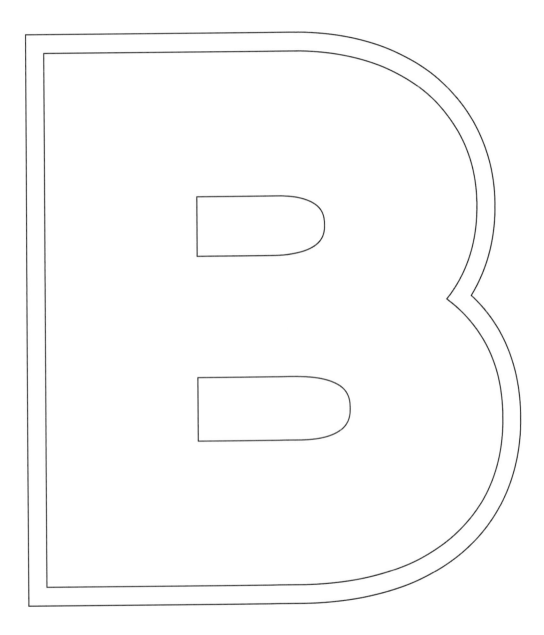

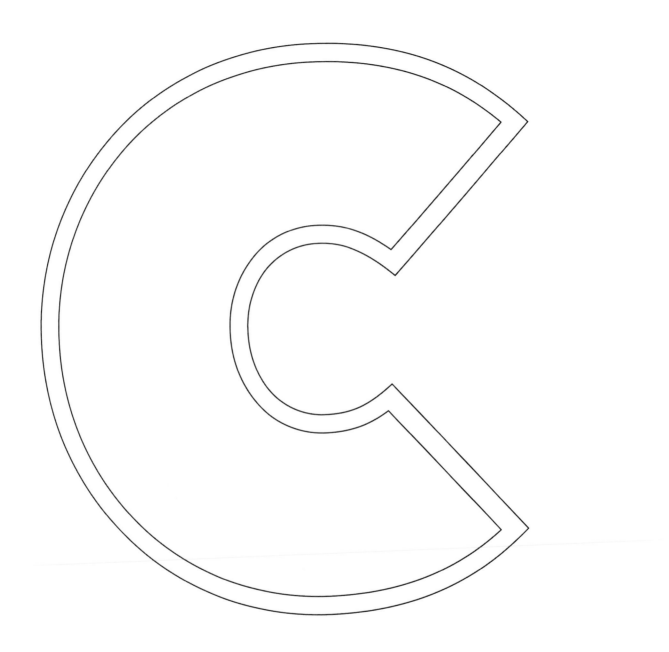

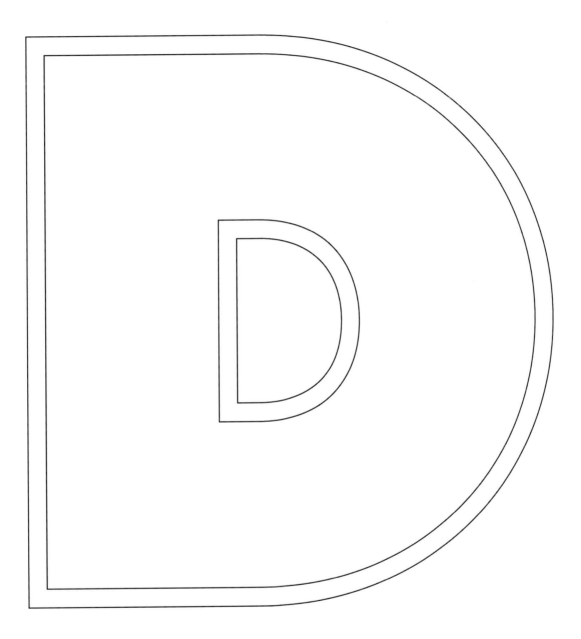

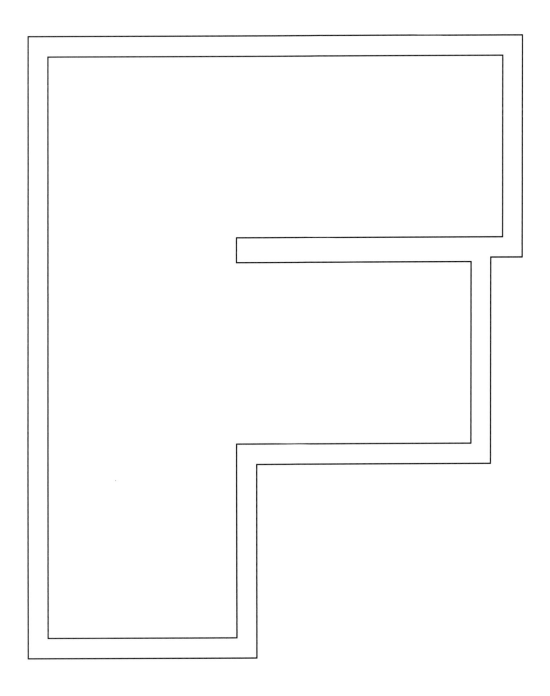

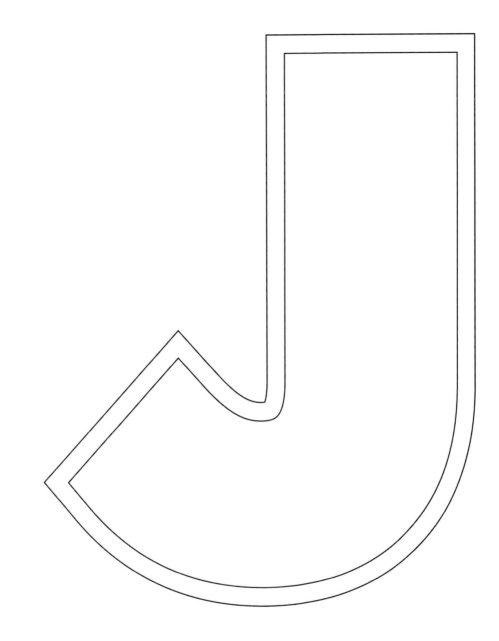

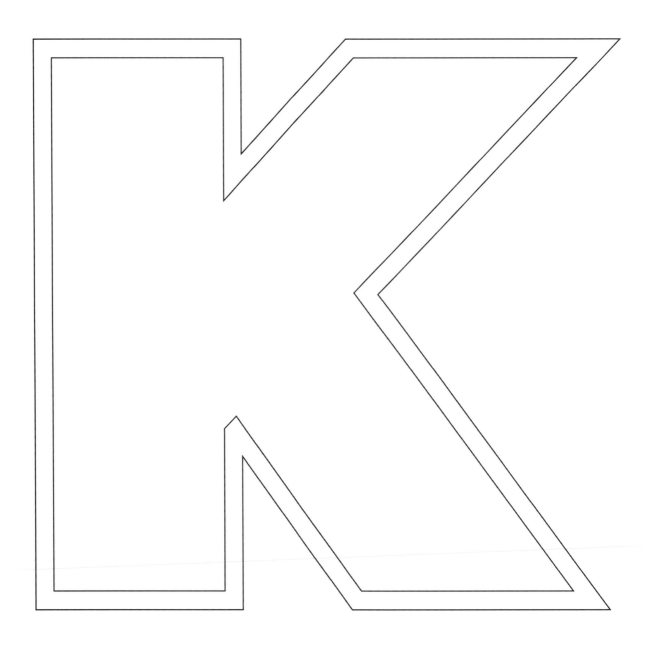

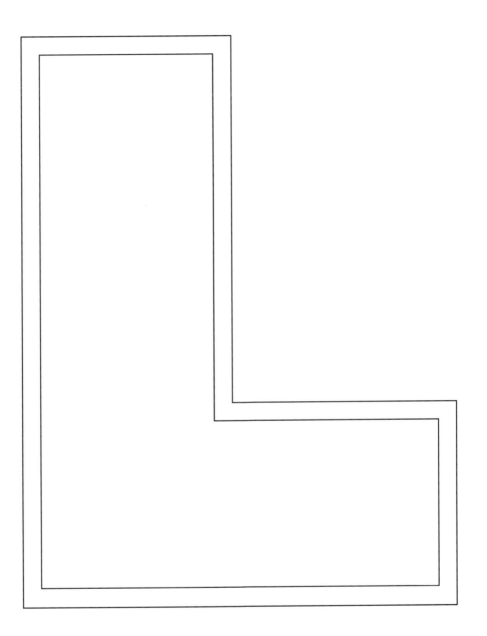

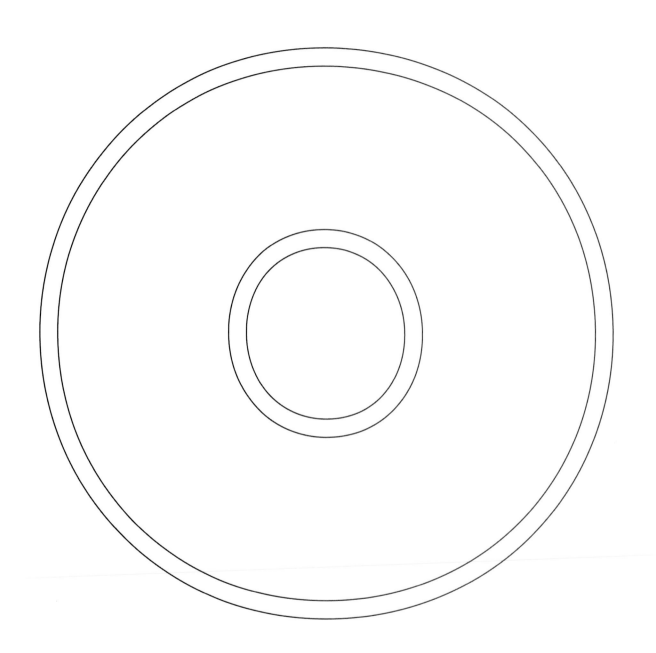

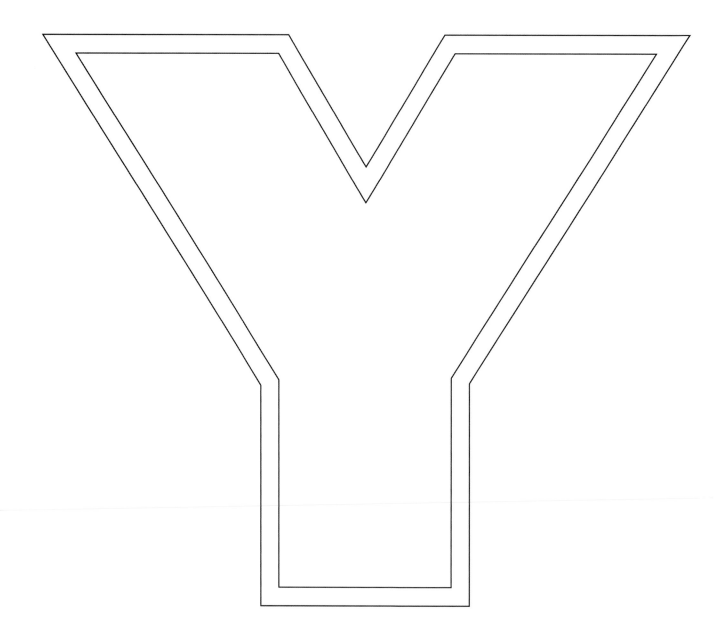

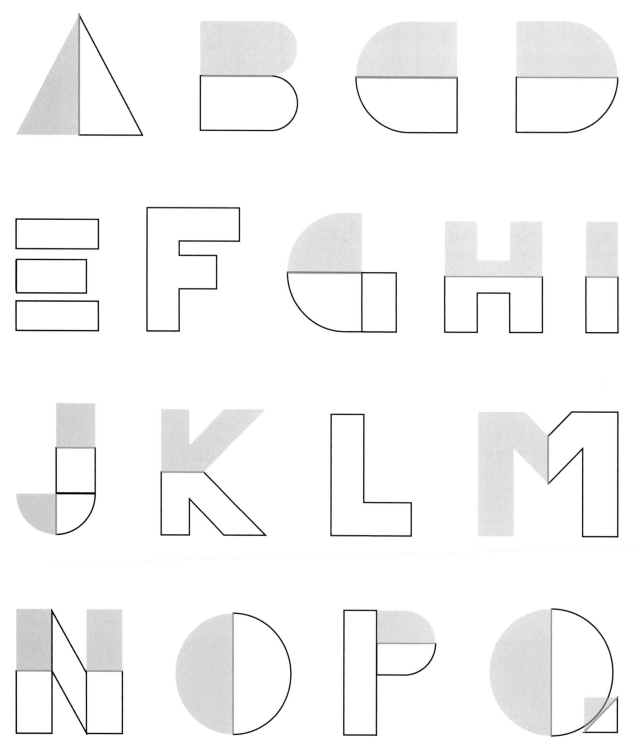

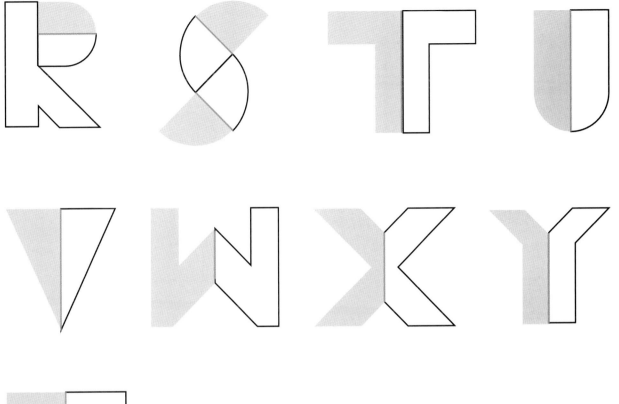

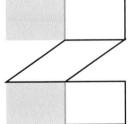

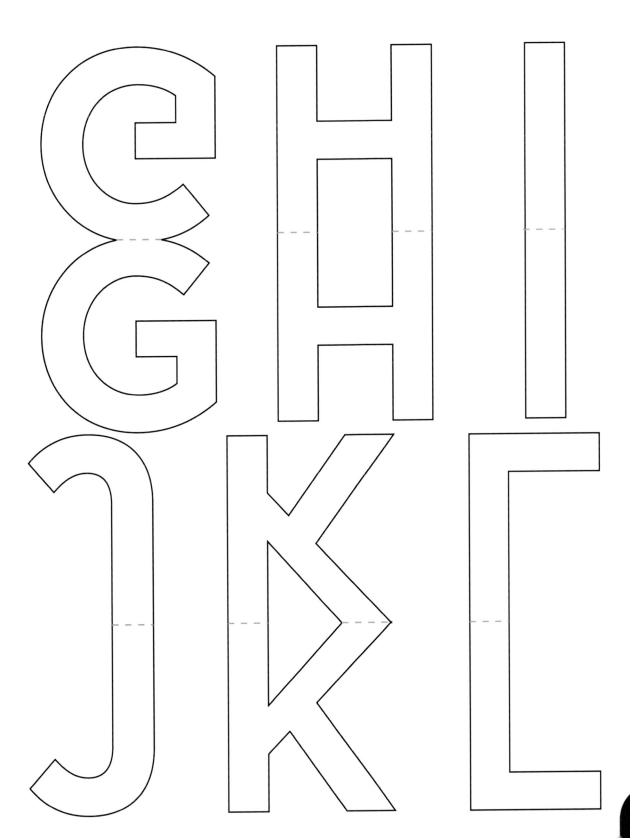

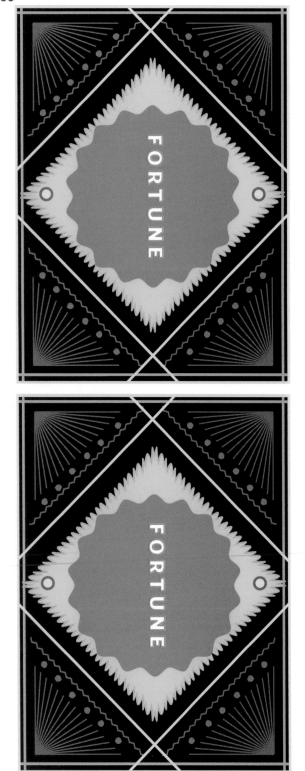

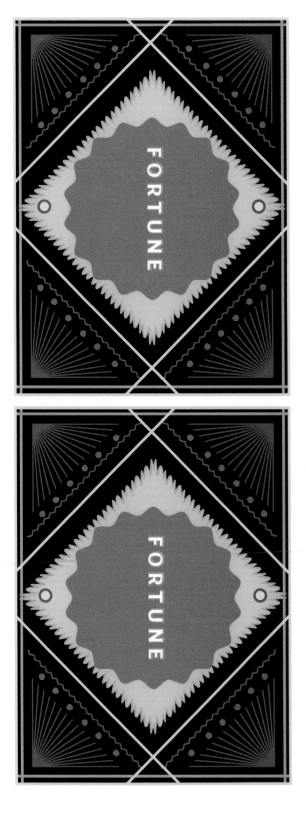

I LOVE YOU
TO THE
MOON
AND BACK.

EAT
DESSERT
FIRST.

ALL YOU NEED IS
SLEEP.

TOMORROW YOU WILL
WAKE UP
WITH A SOCK ON
YOUR FOOT.

233

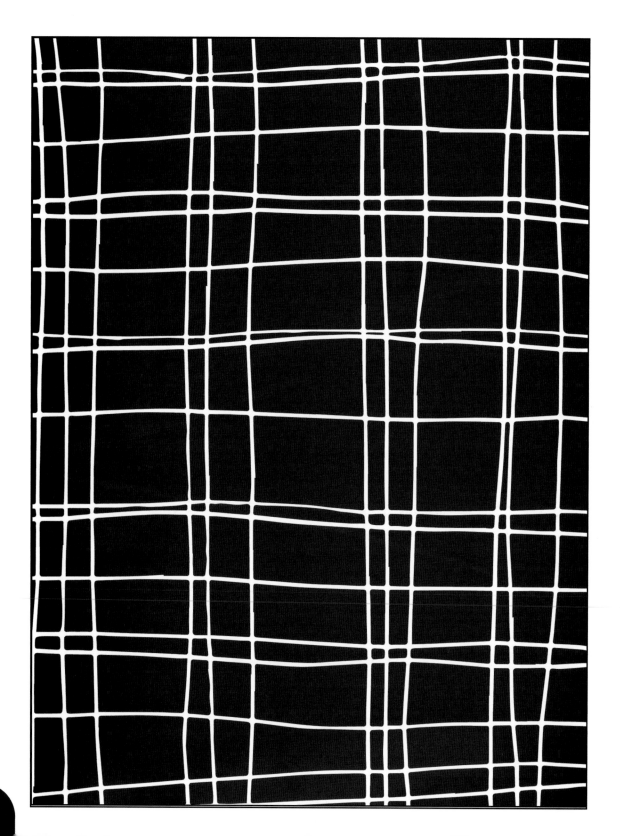

INDEX

ACKNOWLEDGMENTS

This book would not have been possible without the help of my team—Angie Stalker for your spot-on typography and design; Casey Brodley for photographing every image in this book in such beautiful detail; and Julia Wester for your insane crafting and styling skills. I am so proud of the hard work you have all put into this book and that I get to work with you every day.

To my agent, Andy McNicol; my editor, Cassie Jones; and my mentor, Jane Buckingham, for believing in this project before I even knew it was possible.

Special thanks to Sara Tso for consulting on the cake and cookie recipes, Tina Choi for your amazing hand skills and assistance, and Tuna the Frenchie for being the best Oh Joy! pup model.

Finally, to my husband, Bob, daughter, Ruby, and baby girl (who was in my belly when we made this book)—thank you for inspiring me daily with your support and making my life more whimsical and colorful by simply being you.

ABOUT THE AUTHOR

BONNIE TSANG

Joy Cho is the founder and creative director of Oh Joy!—which includes various licensed product lines (including Target and the Land of Nod), how-to lifestyle videos, and a daily blog with a focus on design, fashion, food, and the joyful moments of everyday life. She is the author of two other books and has consulted for hundreds of creative businesses around the world. Joy lives in Los Angeles with her husband and two daughters.

See more at ohjoy.com.